Best of 4 blocks . . .

AND *MORE*

Linda Giesler Carlson

Located in Paducah, Kentucky, the American Quilter's Society (AQS) is dedicated to promoting the accomplishments of today's quilters. Through its publications and events, AQS strives to honor today's quiltmakers and their work and to inspire future creativity and innovation in quiltmaking.

EDITORS: SHELLEY HAWKINS AND DIANNE NELSON
GRAPHIC DESIGN: LYNDA SMITH
COVER DESIGN: MICHAEL BUCKINGHAM
QUILT PHOTOGRAPHY: CHARLES R. LYNCH (unless otherwise noted)

Library of Congress Cataloging-in-Publication Data

Carlson, Linda Giesler.
  Best of four blocks...and more / by Linda Giesler Carlson
    p. cm.
    ISBN 1-57432-828-X
  1. Patchwork--Patterns. 2. Quilting--Patterns. 3. Patchwork
quilts--United States--History.   I. Title

  TT835.C374115 2003
    746.46041--dc22
                                    2003018978

Additional copies of this book may be ordered from the American Quilter's Society, PO Box 3290, Paducah, KY 42002-3290, or online at www.AQSquilt.com.

Dedication

To my twin sister, Diana, my forever friend.
You always bring out the best in me!

Linda and Diana
Photo by John V. Carlson

Contents

CACTUS ROSE WITH TULIPS VARIATION, 84" x 84", ca. 1860. Made by Mrs. C. M. May, Amanda, Ohio. From the author's collection. An antique quilt dealer in Vermont called this quilt a Coxcomb appliqué.

Introduction

It was love at first sight with the grand and glorious four-block quilts I saw in Gwen Marston and Joe Cunningham's book, *American Beauties: Rose and Tulip Quilts* (American Quilter's Society, 1988). These quilts were made by the authors, Betty Harriman, and Mary Schafer. The four-block set truly spoke to me because I had often thought I would never live long enough to recreate all the beautiful quilts I had seen in magazines, calendars, books, and quilt shows.

This style/set was achievable with only four blocks. The more I looked for new and antique four-block quilts, the more I realized they possessed a history begging to be explored. My career legacy was found – to be the voice and advocate for the bold and beautiful four-block quilt.

At the Spencer Art Museum in Lawrence, Kansas, I found four-block quilts by Rose Kretsinger and Charlotte Jane Whitehill. These modern quiltmakers' choices of colors and patterns echoed antique four-block quilts found in quilt books and other museums. But to my surprise, there were more nineteenth-century than twentieth-century four-block quilts.

I wondered why this style/set seemed to lose favor in the twentieth century. It couldn't have been an economic issue, as it may have been in the nineteenth century, to purchase 30" to 45" wide background fabrics, or the need to purchase foreground fabrics for appliqué motifs to fill the larger background blocks. My answer today, as in the early 1990s, is that this was not the most popular quilt style/set made before 1900 and in the states admitted to the Union before 1850. This is evidenced by the small number of these quilts documented by state quilt search projects, as well as those in the possession of antique quilt dealers and museums. It seems that fewer quiltmakers then, and at least in the first half of the twentieth century, were enamored with the big and bold pieced/appliquéd four-block motifs. The majority preferred the more delicate or dainty features in simple or complex multiple-block quilts.

The common threads between the two centuries' four-block quilts were color and pattern choices. The most popular color choices were red and green, bright pink, yellow, and blue. The most common patterns were the flower-filled urns, Princess (or Prince's) Feather, Whig Rose (or Rose of Sharon), and Tree of Life. While they have all enjoyed template variations over their 170-year use, they are still readily recognizable patterns. Since *Roots, Feathers & Blooms* was published in 1994, I have found several more Blazing Star quilts, ca. 1890 to 1920, that could be considered a fifth most popular four-block motif.

Considering the dates of construction and provenance led me to wonder if this style/set had naturally evolved after the whole-cloth quilt and medallion styles, and before the multi-block quilt. I wondered if the patterns came from a particular ethnicity. In 1988, I started my hunt for the ancestral grand and glorious four-block quilts in various publications, archival material, and museums. By 1992, several state quilt search projects opened their files and allowed me to duplicate slides of many of their four-block quilts.

I am grateful to all the project directors and volunteers for finding and sharing their states' quilts and treasured accompanying stories. I would also like to thank all the antique quilt dealers who have contacted me over the past 10 years to report undocumented four-block quilts.

Among the documented quilts, this style/set still remains low in numbers compared to all the variations of other quilt styles/sets, such as the Log Cabin. It is interesting that many of the makers' names that are documented or written on the quilts are Pennsylvania-German in heritage. Many of these

quilts are not worn out and ragged, but are in wonderful condition owing to their favored status in being seldom used. It seems that the more numerous, non-four-block-set quilts were used for everyday linens and not for show when company came.

Because my previous books, *Roots, Feathers & Blooms* and *Four Blocks Continued...*, are out of print, I have received many inquiries as to where they can be found. I have found some copies on the Internet at substantial prices. As an alternative, I thought it was time to update my research and give the loyal four-block quiltmakers some new patterns. *Best of Four Blocks...and More* is a labor of love to show old and new friends how timeless and timely, how grand and glorious, and how bold and beautiful four-block quilts can be.

HETTIE'S WASHINGTON PLUME, 74" x 86", 1928–32. Made by Hettie McBride Campbell. Owned by Charlotte Freels Duvall. Documentation forms from Florida revealed no nineteenth-century four-block quilts and only this one twentieth-century quilt, which didn't fit my criteria. However, it seems appropriate to include a few twentieth-century quilts because they led me to research their origins in the nineteenth century. Photo by Richard Walker.

Charlotte and Hettie

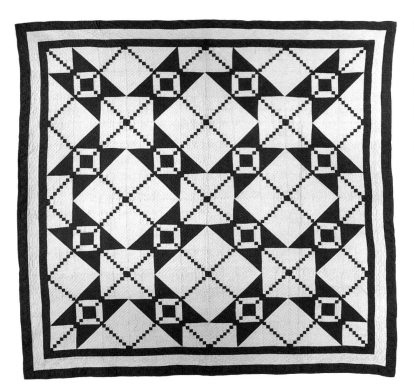

SUSPENDED ROYAL STARS, 78" x 78", ca. 1930, Eastern Pennsylvania. From the author's collection. Although this is another stunning twentieth-century example, this quilt reads as a four-block set but is actually made with small units. The author owns another multi-block made into a four-block set quilt and feels they are rare.

THE QUILTING PARTY, 19" x 26⅛", ca. 1854–1875, painter unknown. Twenty-first century quilters gather today, just as in this nineteenth-century scene. Courtesy of Abby Aldrich Rockefeller Folk Art Museum, Colonial Williamsburg Foundation, Williamsburg, Virginia.

Chapter 1

Four-Block Quilt
designs **AND** *their origins*

Tulip Designs

One of the designs frequently found on quilts made during the blossoming of four-block quilts in America had its roots one ocean, half a continent, and three centuries away. Turkey provided sixteenth-century Europe with tulips, one of the flowers that would eventually grow on four-block quilts. Single bulbs commanded enormous prices during the "tulip mania" of the 1630s.[1]

Women wanting to bring a little of their homeland with them packed a few bulbs among their belongings when immigrating to America, or paid dearly for them when the merchant ship arrived. Well suited to the climates of the northern colonies, tulips became Holland's lucrative export to America in the 1700s. Women grew these colorful flowers and preserved them for posterity in their hearts, their minds, and their quilts.

The tulip as a quilt design became especially popular with Pennsylvania and South Carolina German quiltmakers, who depicted this flower as often or perhaps even more often than the ever-popular rose. Pfalz, now in the state of Rhineland-Pfalz in Bavaria, was the homeland of many emigrants who arrived in Philadelphia. From the Rhine, Baden, and Wurttemberg states of Germany came many emigrants who settled in the Dutch Fork area of South Carolina.[2] In these areas, Fraktur decoration adorned legal documents such as birth, wedding, and death certificates. These designs became popular motifs for pictorial embroidery and weaving. Fraktur painting embellished furniture, wedding chests, and decorated ceramics, as well as painted hex signs above barn doors to protect the farm animals from witches' spells or the feared "evil eye."

In quiltmaking, bulbous tulips with pointed petals were the most often used motifs from Fraktur. Hearts, vines, perched birds, facing or kissing birds (especially on a wedding quilt), astronomical objects, and the round, colorful hex signs with simple floral or geometric designs were used as well, often executed in the favored colors of red, yellow, blue, and green.

A common way to display tulips on quilts was to place these flowers and a variety of others in an urn or vase. Several state quilt documentation projects found four-block urn quilts filled with tulips, roses, coxcombs, currants, and cherries.

URN WITH COXCOMBS AND TULIPS, 84" x 84", 1904. Signed Mary Eliza Sikes. Purchased in Iowa by the author. Photo by Richard Walker.

URN WITH FLOWERS AND CURRANTS, 84" x 84", 1840. Made by Lavina Frick. From the author's collection. Ms. Frick was born in 1827 and completed this quilt when she was 13 years old. Note the piping next to the binding. Photo by Richard Walker.

Lavina Frick

Princess Feather Designs

The pattern we today call Princess Feather, often appearing in a four-block setting, may have originally been named the Prince's Feather or the Prince of Wales Feather. In 1301, King Edward I of Great Britain invested his son, the future Edward II, with the title Prince of Wales. Each succeeding eldest son was likewise invested before accepting the British

JESTER'S PLUME/PRINCESS FEATHER, 83" x 83", made in Indiana ca. 1860–1880. From the author's collection. This may have been a wedding quilt because it has numerous hearts in the quilting. Photo by Richard Walker.

crown. In a letter to me from C. Stevens, curator of the Welsh Folk Museum in Wales, he relates that according to the *Oxford Companion to Welsh Literature*, the motto of the Prince of Wales, *Ich Dien* (German for "I serve"), together with three white ostrich feathers, form the prince's insignia.

The prince's feather insignia, which is still used today, was first depicted on drawings and paintings as three feathers spewing above but attached to the center of a crown worn by the prince. Artist Robert Peake immortalized Henry, Prince of Wales, in about 1610, wearing such a triple-plumed headdress.[3]

C. Stevens comments further about the Prince of Wales Feather quilt pattern: "This is not a motif which figures in Welsh quilting. It is a royal motif pertaining to the Prince of Wales, and is, I believe,

Whig Rose, 63" x 78", made in Iowa before 1860. From the author's collection. In addition to a four-block quilt, this could also be categorized as a transition quilt because of its two half-blocks. Photo by Richard Walker.

Germanic in origin, having no Welsh significance whatsoever!" After 1714, when German George I ascended to the British throne, German decorative goods found their way to the colonies as a result of the English Navigation Acts.[4] In the last quarter of the nineteenth century, the Franklin College of Pennsylvania was established to educate Germans in English culture and taste.[5]

A quilt titled Soldier's Plume was found by the Kentucky Quilt Project and featured two feathers arcing away from a central flower. Considering these various feather patterns and their names, Jonathan Holstein, quilt scholar and author, has designated the set of triple feathers as Prince of Wales Feathers and the single running feather spray as the Princess Feather. Conversations with Welsh quiltmakers have confirmed this distinction.

Rose Designs

The rose, originating in Japan and China, made its way to England and France via trade ships as early as medieval times. Rose varieties were depicted on wool tapestries of the Middle Ages and adorned the glazed and unglazed cotton chintzes that were made in England and France and imported to the American colonies.

During the mid-eighteenth and nineteenth centuries, rose-patterned chintzes were stitched to backings or cut out and appliquéd on linen or cotton to create early American whole-cloth and medallion-style quilts. The North Carolina project found many fine examples of these quilts.

As these styles faded in popularity and the repeated block quilt dominated, roses never failed to bloom. Many rose patterns continued to be found on quilts, particularly those made by women of English or Scots-Irish heritage. Rainfall almost every day of the rose-growing season in the United Kingdom gave birth to the still celebrated English rose gardens.

Colonials and later immigrants appliquéd them on their "new garden beds." The most popular four-block rose pattern was the Whig Rose, which has also been known as the Rose of Sharon.

Other Flower Designs

Even flowers that were considered weeds in some countries found their way to four-block quilts. The Thistle pattern came from Scotland, where it was a royal insignia, created in 1452 by James II for men inducted into knighthood. The K.T. initials after their names meant "Knight of the Thistle." This woody, prickly scrub plant is extremely hearty and tenacious and stands for unity and pride. Women of Scots heritage remembered this symbol of courage and tenacity in the face of adversity by stitching it on their quilts in a new land.

Although not often seen, the ancient Egyptian Lotus pattern looks very akin to the thistle and is often confused with it. Another flower similar to the thistle is the coxcomb, which was often found in urns or vases in the large four-block quilts. Both the Lotus and Coxcomb patterns could well be variations of the Thistle. I have found these three names to be interchangeable on very similar four-block quilts and printed patterns.

Tree of Life Designs

The other popular four-block pattern found with some regularity is the Tree of Life design. This pattern emerged as a chintz central medallion motif in the mid-eighteenth to the mid-nineteenth centuries. Several of these Tree of Life medallion quilts were found by the North Carolina Quilt Documentation Project. When created in the four-block set, the Tree of Life motif is not quite as elaborate in leaf, flower, fruit, or bird as its medallion predecessor. Instead of chintzes, solid and print calicoes were used to create the trees and other motifs.

TREE OF LIFE, 80" x 80", ca. 1850–1870. From the author's collection. This quilt has the baby hand prints of Keith and Kenneth in the quilting, which could signify the joy of their birth or mourning of their short lives.

MEREDITH'S TREE OF LIFE AT MIDNIGHT, 80" x 90", 1993. Made by the author for her daughter, Meredith, and quilted by Katie Borntreger, Verona, Missouri. A memorial to the author's father and grandparents is on the back of the quilt. Photo by Richard Walker.

Pieced Designs

Very few pieced four-block quilts have been found in state documentation projects. South Carolina documented more pieced four-block quilts than any other state in my survey. All were made in the last quarter of the nineteenth to early twentieth century, and most often, four stars were depicted. Blazing Star was a common pattern, although several eight-pointed stars were seen. Some pieced four-block quilt patterns, such as the Carolina Lily pattern, included a small amount of appliqué. Rocky Mountain pattern quilts were also found, and two quilts featured four large Xs. Only rarely did some pieced original patterns surface, but a few that did are spectacular.

MENNONITE POSTAGE STAMP STARS, 82" x 82", made in York County, Pennsylvania, ca. 1875. From the author's collection.

Chapter 2

Gallery
of four-block quilts

The four-block quilts shown in this gallery are wonderful examples of the stunning results that can be achieved when this large-block format is used.

POT OF COXCOMB, 80" x 84", made in Indiana ca. 1860–1880. Purchased in Iowa by the author. Photo by Richard Walker.

SAWTOOTH SQUARE IN A SQUARE, 89" x 90", ca. 1850–1900. This antique quilt was found in Vermont. From the author's collection.

BEST OF FOUR BLOCKS…AND MORE *Linda Giesler Carlson*

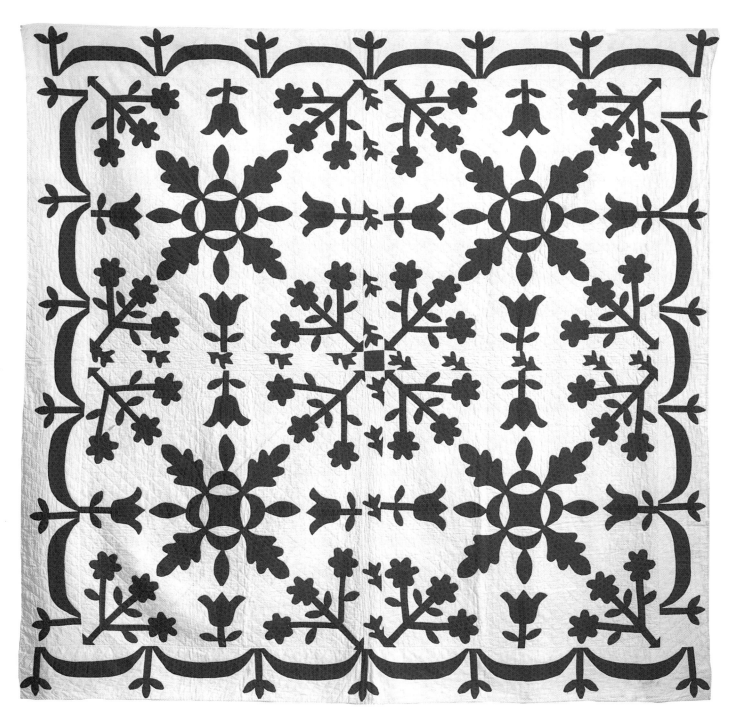

OAK LEAF & REEL WITH TULIPS, 82½" x 82½", made in Pennsylvania ca. 1880s, purchased in Iowa. From the author's collection. Oak leaves, reels, and tulips were combined in this traditional red and white antique quilt.

PERSIAN PICKLE FEATHER, 66" x 66", 1999. Made by the author. This quilt showcases two of the author's workshops, "Beautiful Backgrounds" and "Feather Borders for Everyone."

ROSE OF SHARON WREATH, 84" x 84", made in Anson County, North Carolina, ca. 1850 by Emma Barrett. From the author's collection. See page 95 for the author's replication and quilt pattern.

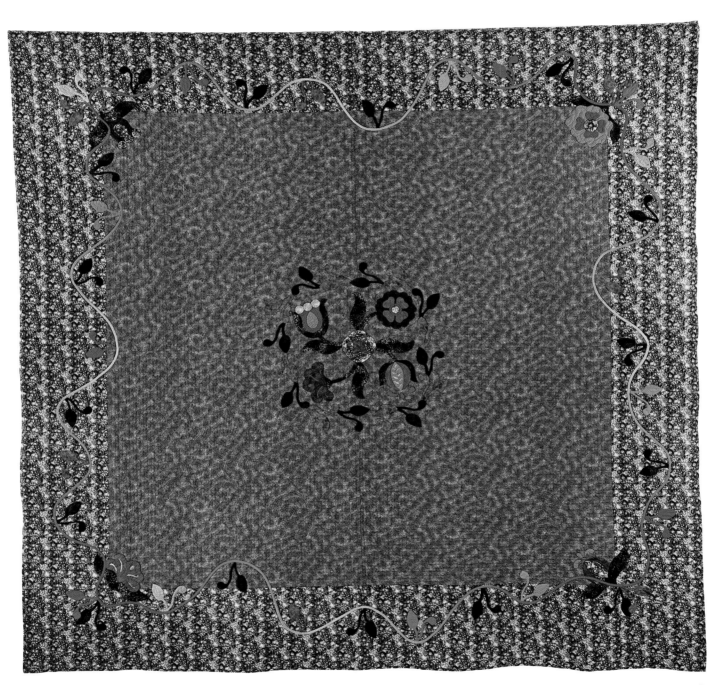

FOUR-BLOCK WHOLECLOTH MEDALLION, 92" x 92", 1996. Made by the author. The floral quilting lines were drawn on the blocks before sewing them together, then the center floral lines were drawn, and finally, the crosshatching. The appliqué motifs were added, then borders sewn before the final border appliqué was added.

Chapter 3

General

supplies AND directions

The following supplies and directions are detailed here and should be considered for all pattern instructions:

Basic Sewing Kit

Paper and fabric scissors; small, very sharp scissors for scherenschnitte

Freezer paper and template plastic

Appliqué needles (I prefer #11 sharps)

Quilting needles (I prefer #10 or #11 betweens)

Thimble

Threads to match fabrics

Fabric markers and pencils

Rulers: 18" to 24" in length and a square ruler 6" or larger with a diagonal line

Compass for quilting designs (optional)

Rotary cutter with a new blade

Rotary cutting mat

Sewing machine with accurate ¼" seam allowance guide

Fabric

Prewash and iron all fabric before use, to guard against color bleeding and excessive shrinkage.

Template Patterns

All template patterns, except for those that are machine pieced, do not have seam allowances included. You will need to cut the patterns about ⅛" away from your traced line on the fabric.

Machine piecing: Use an accurate ¼" seam allowance guide. For NORTH, EAST, SOUTH & WEST, MY CAPTAIN IS THE BEST (page 114), a seam allowance is included on the patterns. My secret to accurate machine piecing is to use a ¹⁄₁₆" hole punch to mark the sewing line in the seam allowance on the template plastic. Remember to place a dot inside each hole when tracing around them on the fabric. These dots are the pinning and sewing line guides.

Sawtooth Squares

1. Match the two fabrics with right sides together and raw edges perfectly aligned. Yardage requirements are given in the pattern directions.

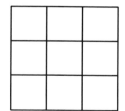

2. Draw a grid of squares, as per pattern directions.

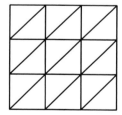

3. Draw diagonal lines through each grid square.

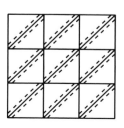

4. Sew exactly ¼" away from both sides of the diagonal lines. Pick up the foot at each horizontal line, cut your threads, and start again on the next diagonal line.

5. After sewing, cut the squares apart on all drawn lines: horizontal, diagonal, and vertical. Lightly press the sawtooth squares open.

6. Using a ¼" seam, sew the number of squares together as indicated in the pattern directions. Be sure to alternate the sawtooth colors.

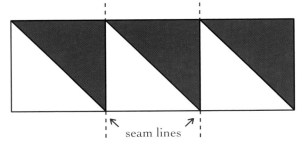

seam lines

Flying Geese Squares

1. Cut the number of units 1 and 2 as indicated in the pattern instructions.

2. With right sides together, pin two of Unit 2 (background squares) on Unit 1.

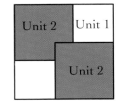

3. With a ruler, draw a diagonal line through each Unit 2. On both sides of the diagonal line, stitch an accurate ¼" seam.

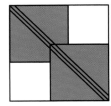

4. Cut the units apart on the diagonal line, forming two pieces.

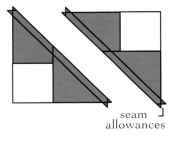

seam allowances

5. On one of the new pieces, finger press or iron Unit 2 with the seam allowances away from Unit 1.

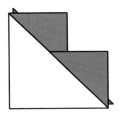

6. With right sides together, pin another Unit 2 to the lower left corner of the Unit 1. Draw a diagonal line through the new Unit 2.

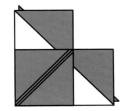

7. Stitch ¼" away from both sides of the diagonal line. Cut the unit apart on the diagonal line. Finger press open. Two finished Flying Geese units are formed.

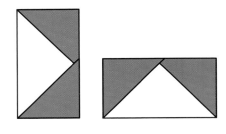

8. Repeat with the remaining units.

9. Join the number of Flying Geese units as indicated in the pattern instructions.

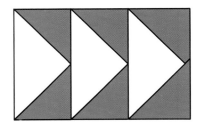

The directions for the machine-pieced Flying Geese are reprinted courtesy of Ken and Shirley Wengler, Newberry, Florida.

Machine-Applied Binding

Self-made or purchased binding can be used. I prefer a double-fold bias binding made from one of the fabrics in the quilt. To make the binding, cut 2¼" wide strips. Sew end to end with a diagonal seam, then fold the entire length in half, wrong sides together, and press.

Applying the binding: On the right side of the finished quilt, about 6" away from a corner, place and pin the raw edges of the binding against the raw edge of the quilt.

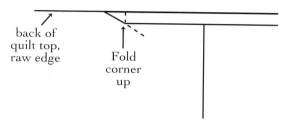

back of
quilt top,
raw edge

Fold
corner
up

Fold the beginning edge of the binding up to form a 45-degree angle. Begin stitching, stopping ¼" away from the corner. Backstitch to secure threads, then cut them. Lift the machine foot to reposition the quilt before continuing to the next corner.

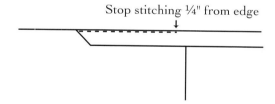

Stop stitching ¼" from edge

Now, lift and fold the loose end of the binding to a 45-degree angle.

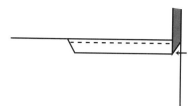

Next, fold the binding back over the folded angle so that the second fold is even with the edge of the quilt. Pin to the side of the quilt.

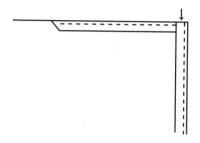

Position the needle back into the ¼" tacking. Take two stitches, then backstitch before continuing in the same manner on the remaining sides and corners. Repeat for each corner.

Overlap the binding and stitch a couple of inches past the beginning. Fold the binding to the back of the quilt and stitch in place by hand.

Chapter 4

Four-Block
quilt projects

The patterns presented in this book reflect outstanding quilts found during my research, as well as examples of the four most commonly found four-block quilt designs. All of these designs are my original interpretations, with the exception of COXCOMB CROSSING, which is a slightly changed reproduction of an unnamed antique quilt.

Both piecing and appliqué techniques are used in the patterns, which are geared to the intermediate for advanced quiltmaker. Some patterns, such as AMY'S WEDDING QUILT, require piecing in certain sections of the block. COXCOMB CROSSING is entirely pieced and requires some curved piecing of leaves to background pieces. The design is then appliquéd onto the background block.

Before you begin making your own four-block quilt, prewash and iron all fabrics. Be sure to position and draw around piecing templates on the wrong side of the fabric and trace around the appliqué templates on the right side of the fabric. The needle-turn method of appliqué is the easiest and quickest for me.

You are about to embark on an exciting project. It can be rich in symbolism or simply a decorative heirloom to pass on to future generations. Remember, there are only four blocks!

Butterfly

Scherenschnitte

BUTTERFLY SCHERENSCHNITTE, 80" x 80", 1999. Made by the author for two of her workshops, titled "Paperdolls, Snowflakes, and Scherenschnitte" and "Beautiful Backgrounds: Fabric and Quilting Choices." Often after joining the four blocks together, there is room in the center for a special appliqué or quilting motif.

Fabric and Cutting Requirements

4 yards for (4) 32½" background squares

4 yards for (4) 32½" squares for A

2½ yards for (4) 8½" x 81¼" borders

(1) 20" square for B

(1) 18" x 90" strip for C

(1) 30" square for 32 D and Dr

(2) 7" square scraps for two full-sized E

(1) 7" square scrap for two half-sized E

(2) 6" square scraps for F

(1) 27" square for 12 G and 1" x 260" bias vines

1 yard for 2¼" x 330" (eight strips 2¼" x 44")
    bias binding

Supplies

Basic sewing kit, page 21

(1) 32" square paper

(1) 20" square paper

(1) 12" x 18" and (1) 8½" x 11" tracing paper

Freezer paper

Stapler

Small, very sharp paper scissors

Metallic and variegated rayon or cotton quilting
    threads (optional)

Batting for 80" square

Backing for 80" square

Block Assembly

1. Fold the 32" square paper in half to form a rectangle. Keep the fold on the bottom. Fold in half again, right side over left, to make quarter folds. Mark the center fold with an asterisk. To make eighths, fold the quarter square into a triangle as shown. Keep the center fold asterisk on the bottom 90-degree angle.

2. Join and trace all dotted and solid lines of the Butterfly Scherenschnitte A pattern with a pencil onto 12" x 18" tracing paper, noting the center fold with an asterisk.

3. Turn the traced A pattern over and align the center fold asterisks of the pattern and the 32" paper triangle. Match all edges of the pattern to the paper and trace the lines, pressing firmly so the pencil line will rub off onto the folded paper.

Remove the tracing paper and darken the traced lines. Staple the new Butterfly Scherenschnitte folded paper pattern together.

4. Before cutting, mark areas to be cut out with a star. The secret to cutting scherenschnitte is to move the pattern, not your hand holding the scissors, to turn corners. Turn only with your free hand to ensure accuracy and minimize the shifting of inner papers. Start cutting out the outside solid line only, then the smaller inner areas of the design while you have more of the pattern to hold onto.

5. When all solid-line areas are cut out, unfold the pattern. Pin and trace onto one of the 32½" squares of fabric for A. Repeat for the remaining three squares.

6. Center the traced design over the 32½" background squares. Baste.

7. Starting in the center of the block and only doing a few inches at a time, cut ⅛" or less away from traced lines on the top fabric and needle-turn appliqué.

8. Repeat steps 6 and 7 for remaining three blocks.

9. Sew two sets of two blocks, right sides together, with an accurate ¼" seam. Sew the two sets of blocks together, matching centers and pinning outward to both ends.

Center Appliqué

1. Fold the 20" square paper in half horizontally, then vertically. Mark the center fold with an asterisk.

2. With a pencil, trace the dotted, solid lines, and center fold asterisk of the Moth Scherenschnitte B pattern onto 8½" x 11" tracing paper. Turn the paper over, matching center asterisk and folds. Firmly trace onto folded 20" paper. Remove tracing paper and darken traced lines. Staple new B pattern together and star areas to be cut out.

3. Cut out as before on solid lines and slit lines that delineate the moths' wings only.

4. Center, pin, and trace the B pattern onto the 20" square fabric.

5. Center the 20" square traced pattern on the center of the quilt top. Baste. Starting in the center of the Moth Scherenschnitte and cutting only a few inches at a time, cut ⅛" or less away from the traced lines on the top fabric and needle-turn appliqué.

Border Assembly

1. Trace the C pattern, Butterfly Body Border Frame, onto the dull side of the freezer paper, marking dotted lines at both ends to indicate folds. Cut out on the lines. Make two or three of these patterns because they will be used 16 times.

2. Read this step entirely before completing. Iron the C freezer paper pattern, waxy side down, onto the 18" x 90" fabric vertically. Trace the pattern on all sides except the ends with the dot-

ted lines. Abut, iron, and trace the pattern end to end to equal four body lengths. You will need four vertical sets of four butterfly bodies that measure 80" in length. Leave ½" space between each vertical set for cutting a ¼" seam allowance the entire 80".

3. Matching long, straight edges, center the butterfly body border frame onto the border and pin from the center to both ends. Baste, then needle-turn appliqué in place. Repeat for the remaining three borders.

4. Match the center of one border to the top of the quilt, pin, and sew. Repeat for bottom of quilt, then the two side borders. Miter the corners.

5. Fold and press the 27" square fabric for the bias vine on the diagonal. With a ruler, trace the fold with a fabric marker on the wrong side. Trace 1" wide diagonal lines on both sides of the fold four more times. Cut on the lines to make eight bias strips. Sew the strips end to end to measure about 260" long.

6. Fold the bias vine wrong sides together and sew with a ¼" seam allowance. Trim the seam allowance to ⅛". Roll the seam to the middle of the tube and iron in place.

7. Trace the D, E, F, and G patterns onto freezer paper as previously described. Cut out on the lines and iron onto the appropriate fabrics. Trace, remove paper, and cut out ⅛" away from the drawn lines.

8. Refer to the quilt photo, page 25, and randomly place the bias vine in an undulating, serpentine fashion, halfway from the adjacent corners toward the centers of each border. Save extra length of the vine. Baste.

9. Position the flowers (G) under the vines, and the various-sized leaves (D) under and over the vines as desired. Place the frogs (F) and half butterflies (E) at the mid-border points. Cut the remaining bias vine into short pieces as needed to connect the leaves to the serpentine vine. Pin and baste in place. Baste flowers, leaves, frogs, and half butterflies in place, then needle-turn appliqué.

10. Pin or baste the full-sized butterflies (E) over the two corners, covering the beginning points of the bias vines. Appliqué.

Finishing

1. Mark quilt as desired.

2. Layer backing, batting, and top. Baste and quilt.

3. Apply binding following the general directions, page 23.

A
Butterfly
Scherenschnitte
block guide

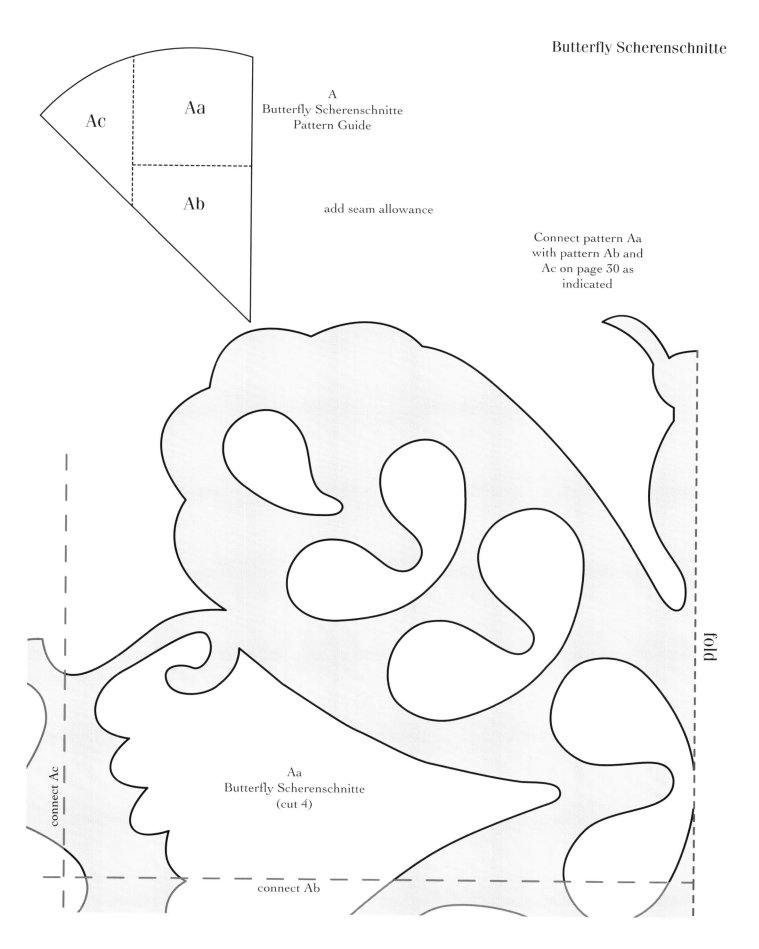

A
Butterfly Scherenschnitte
Pattern Guide

Ac

Aa

Ab

add seam allowance

Connect pattern Aa
with pattern Ab and
Ac on page 30 as
indicated

fold

connect Ac

Aa
Butterfly Scherenschnitte
(cut 4)

connect Ab

Butterfly Scherenschnitte

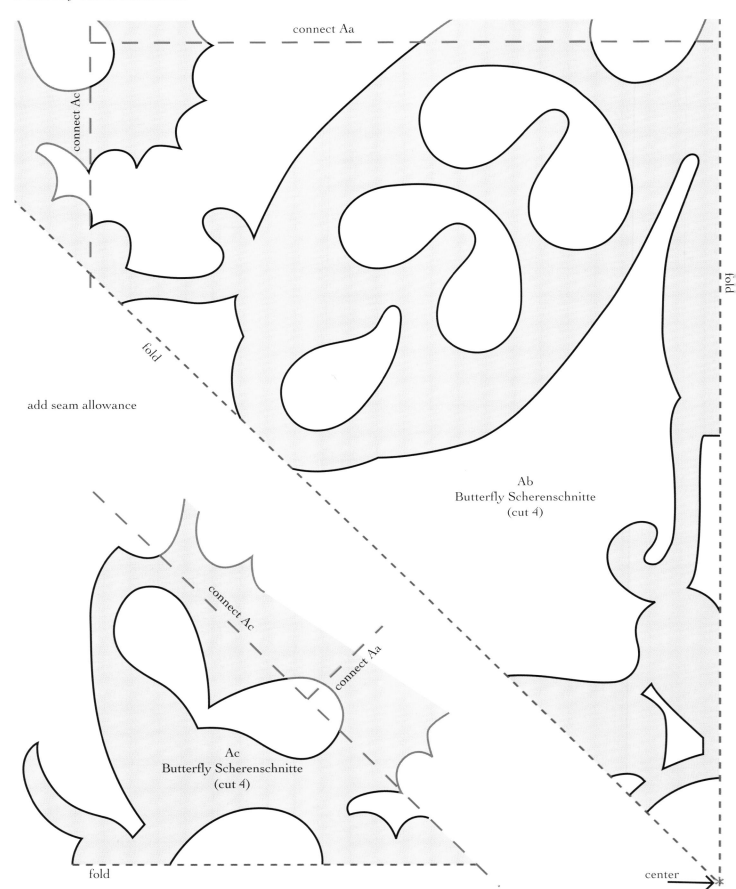

connect Aa

connect Ac

fold

fold

add seam allowance

Ab
Butterfly Scherenschnitte
(cut 4)

connect Ac

connect Aa

Ac
Butterfly Scherenschnitte
(cut 4)

fold

center

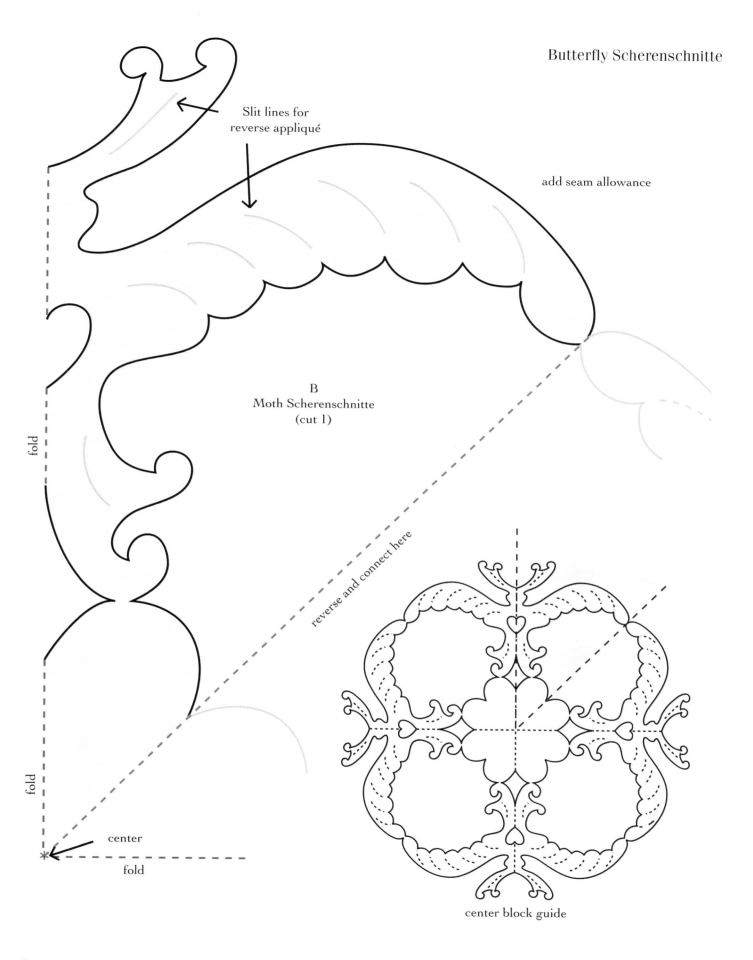

Slit lines for
reverse appliqué

add seam allowance

fold

B
Moth Scherenschnitte
(cut 1)

reverse and connect here

fold

fold

center

fold

center block guide

Butterfly Scherenschnitte

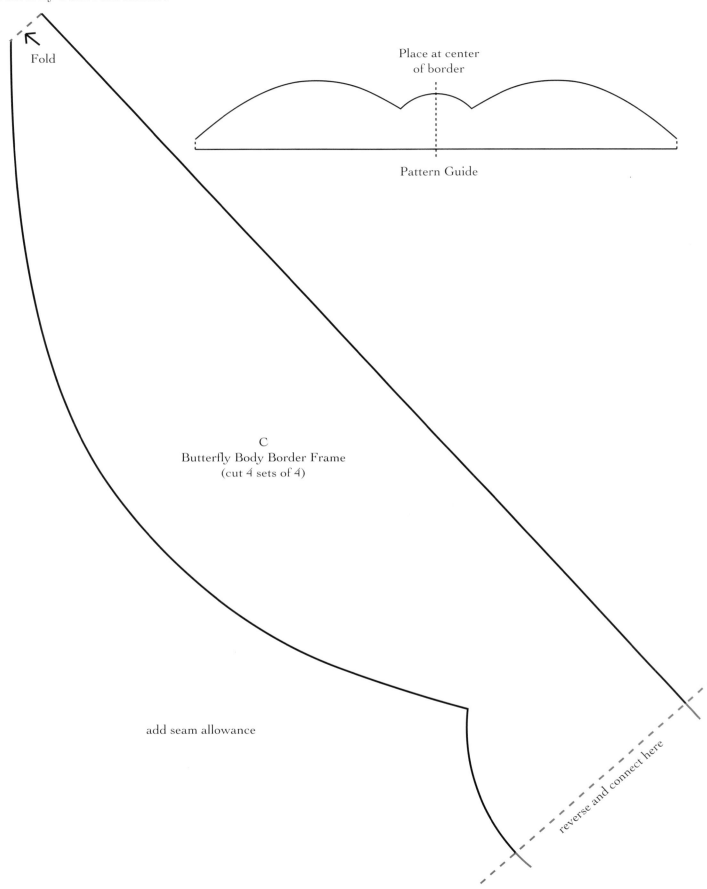

Fold

Place at center
of border

Pattern Guide

C
Butterfly Body Border Frame
(cut 4 sets of 4)

add seam allowance

reverse and connect here

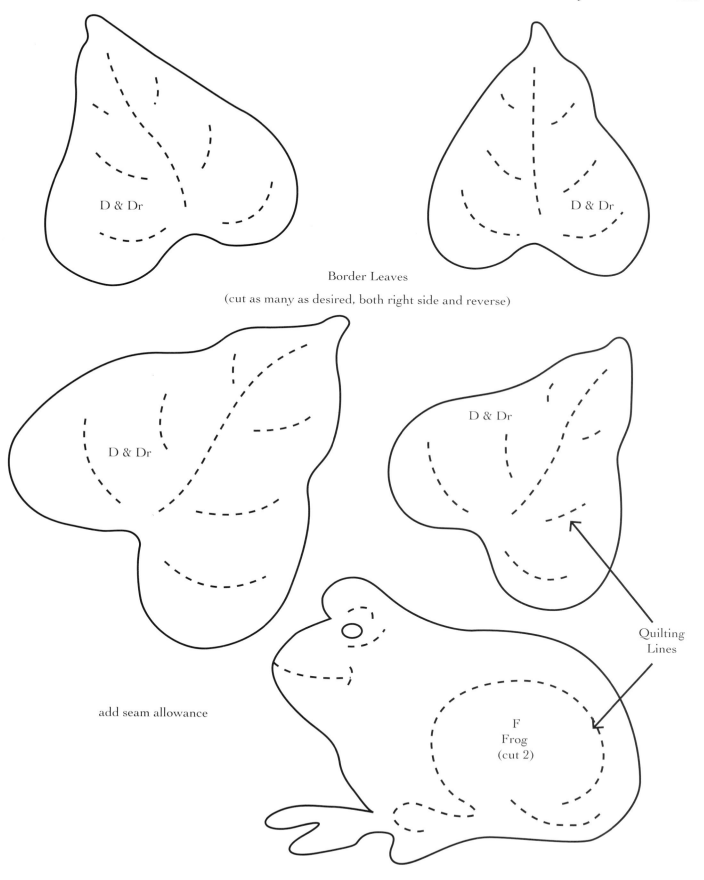

D & Dr

D & Dr

Border Leaves

(cut as many as desired, both right side and reverse)

D & Dr

D & Dr

Quilting
Lines

add seam allowance

F
Frog
(cut 2)

Butterfly Scherenschnitte

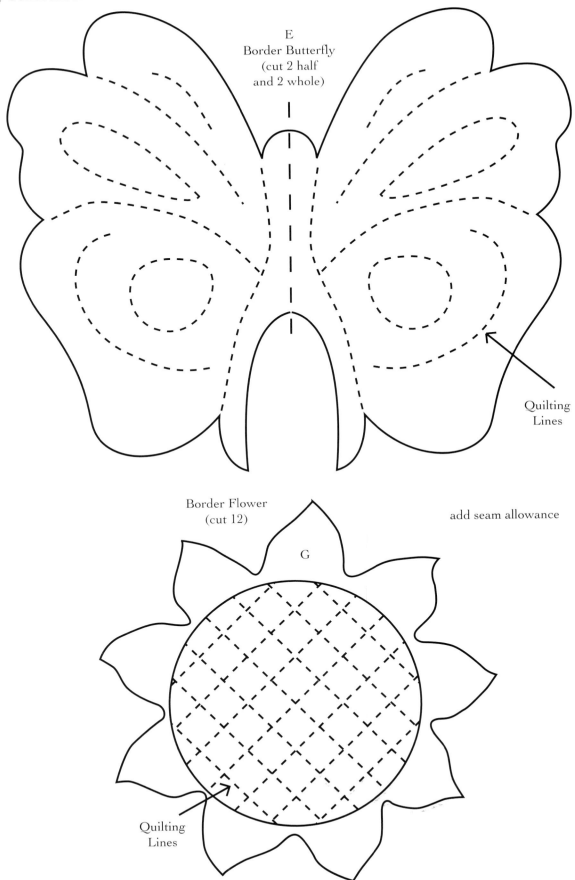

E
Border Butterfly
(cut 2 half
and 2 whole)

Quilting
Lines

Border Flower
(cut 12)

add seam allowance

G

Quilting
Lines

BIRDS ON A VINE, 86" x 86", 1998. Made by the author. With the four appliqué motifs set on point, room is created for a fifth block in the center. Choosing a darker or brighter fabric for the center block creates great visual interest. A bold and unique background is achieved with batik fabric that has a splotchy look, intermixing light and dark areas. Reverse appliqué in the leaves allows the vibrant background to show through. Adding birds and beaded berries on the appliquéd border vines gives the quilt a touch of whimsy and sparkle.

Fabric and Cutting Requirements

4⅛ yards for (4) 34½" background squares

3¼ yards* for (4) 27" appliqué squares

⅞ yard† for (1) 27" center appliqué square

3⅛ yards for (4) 9½" x 86½" borders and

     2¼" x 350" (eight strips 2¼" x 44") binding

1¼ yards for border vines and corner leaves

½ yard for birds and berries

¼ yard for berries

Supplies

Basic sewing kit, page 21

18" wide freezer paper

Small, very sharp scissors

Small, sparkling beads for embellishment

Scrap batting for berries

Batting for 86" square

Backing for 86" square

*For the bird and vine motif, choose highly contrasting fabric from the background.

†Center block fabric should be darker or brighter than other four blocks.

Block Assembly

1. Cut two 18" x 30" sheets of freezer paper. So that you have an approximate 30" square piece, vertically overlap the long edges of the sheets ¼" and iron together.

2. With a heavy line, trace the BIRDS ON A VINE block patterns onto the freezer paper, joining sections as indicated. Cut out on the lines. The pattern will be flimsy, so handle with care.

3. Place the entire freezer-paper motif onto the right side of a 27" block. Iron and trace. The pattern will be used for four more times, so carefully remove the paper and repeat this step for the remaining blocks, including the new fabric for the center block.

4. Center and baste the 27" design onto the 34½" background block. To allow some of the background fabric to show through on the leaves, draw small curved lines that will be cut as you reverse appliqué. Cut an ⅛" seam allowance away from the traced lines about 3" at a time and needle-turn appliqué the design. Repeat for the three background blocks. The center design will be appliquéd when the four blocks are joined.

5. Refer to the photograph on page 35 and join two blocks, right sides together. Repeat for the remaining two blocks. With right sides together, pin both sets, matching center seams first, then pinning outward to the edges. Sew the blocks together.

6. Baste the center design where the four blocks meet in the center of the quilt. Needle-turn appliqué.

Border Assembly

1. Join and trace the BIRDS ON A VINE border appliqué pattern on the dull side of a 40" long sheet of freezer paper. This border vine motif will need to be reversed. Cut the pattern out on the lines.

2. Place the freezer-paper pattern shiny side down onto the right side of the border vine fabric and iron. Trace the design, then remove the paper. Trace three more border vines, then four reversed border vines. Leave ample space between the eight rows of border vines on the 1¼-yard fabric so they can be cut apart.

3. Fold each 86½" border in half, matching the folds with the center of each side of the quilt top. Pin and sew to the quilt top. The borders will extend beyond the quilt body.

4. Miter and sew the corners, cutting the excess corner seam allowance to ¼".

5. Refer to the photograph on page 35 and place one border vine and one reversed border vine on each of the four borders. Baste. Appliqué three single leaves with stems over the four mitered corners.

6. Trace the bird from the block design twice onto the dull side of the freezer paper and cut on the lines. Iron onto the right side of the fabric and trace. Make 16 birds. Cut away ⅛" from the traced lines.

7. Place four birds on each border as desired. Needle-turn appliqué the birds, then appliqué the border vines.

Berry Assembly

1. For small berries, trace a dime or thimble on the right side of the fabric. For medium-sized berries, use a penny or nickel. With a doubled, matching-colored thread, baste ⅛" inside the raw edges. Tightly stuff all berries with batting about twice as large as the circle. Pull the threads tightly. Insert the needle into the tightly gathered neck of the berry twice from opposite sides and knot.

2. To attach sparkling beads, use a thread that matches the bead color. Insert the needle into the center bottom, coming out the center top of the berry. Between thumb and forefinger, flatten the berry, then thread the bead onto the needle. Reinsert the needle into the center top of the berry and pull out through the bottom tightly to hold the bead in place.

3. To attach berries to the quilt, hold in place and insert the needle into the bottom of the berry from the back of the quilt top, coming out in the neck. Repeat twice to secure the berry. Wind thread around the berry three times, then reinsert needle to the back of the quilt and knot.

4. For a cluster of berries, start with the center berry and attach to quilt top as in Step 3. Depending on the size of the berry, you will need to attach more berries around the one in the center. Sew each berry to the next one on the front of the quilt top by inserting the needle in one berry, then into the next one. Knot the thread on the back of the quilt.

Finishing

1. Mark quilt as desired.

2. Layer backing, batting, and top. Baste and quilt.

3. Apply binding following the general directions, page 23.

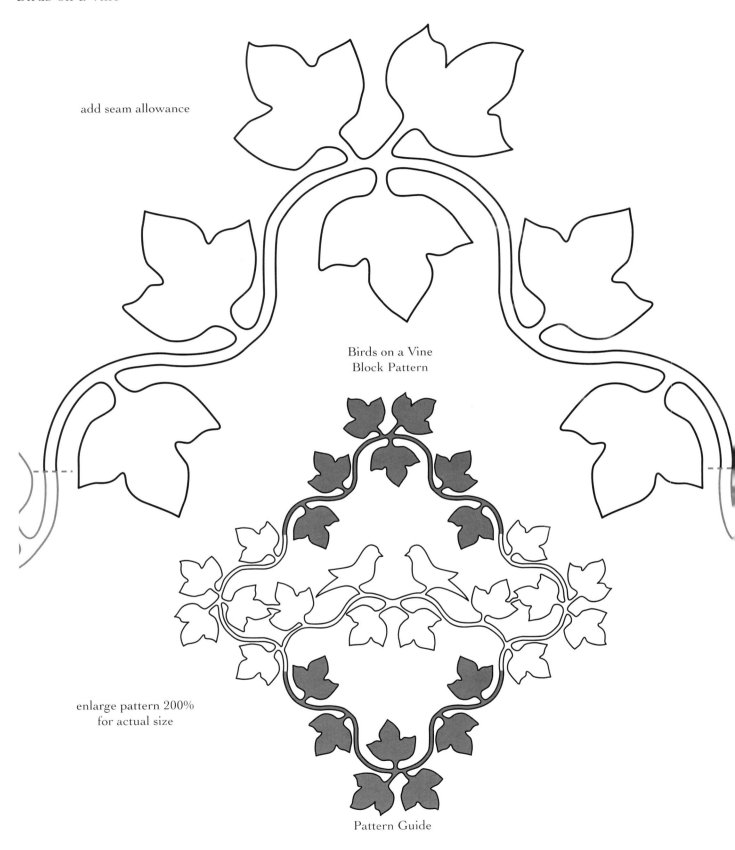

add seam allowance

Birds on a Vine
Block Pattern

enlarge pattern 200%
for actual size

Pattern Guide

BEST OF FOUR BLOCKS…AND MORE *Linda Giesler Carlson*

Birds on a Vine
Block Pattern

reverse
pattern
here

enlarge pattern 200%
for actual size

add seam allowance

Pattern Guide

BEST OF FOUR BLOCKS...AND MORE *Linda Giesler Carlson*

Birds on a Vine

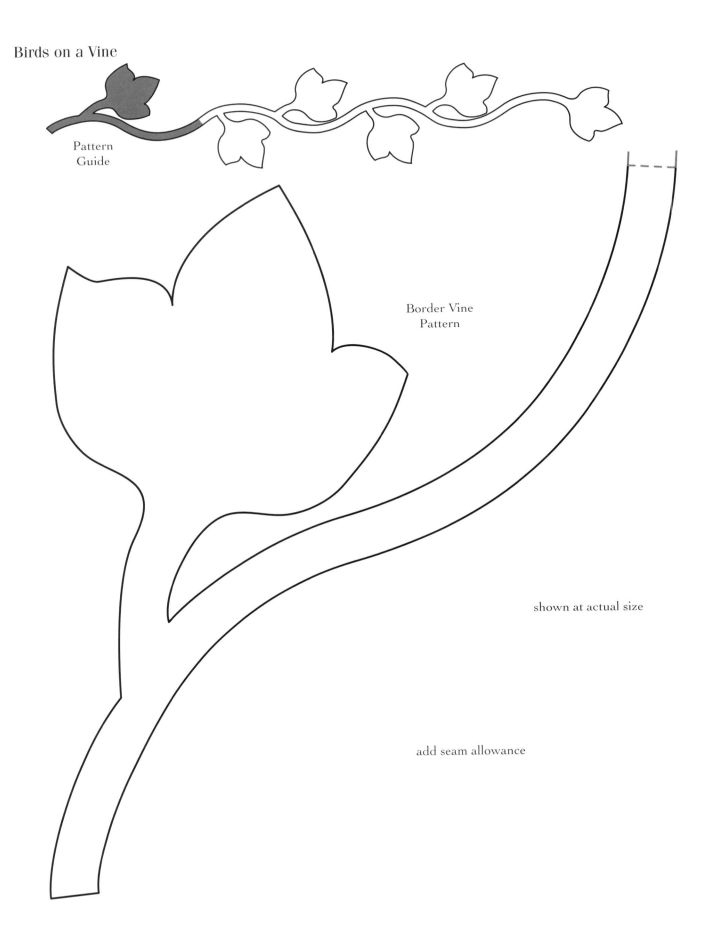

Pattern Guide

Border Vine Pattern

shown at actual size

add seam allowance

BEST OF FOUR BLOCKS...AND MORE *Linda Giesler Carlson*

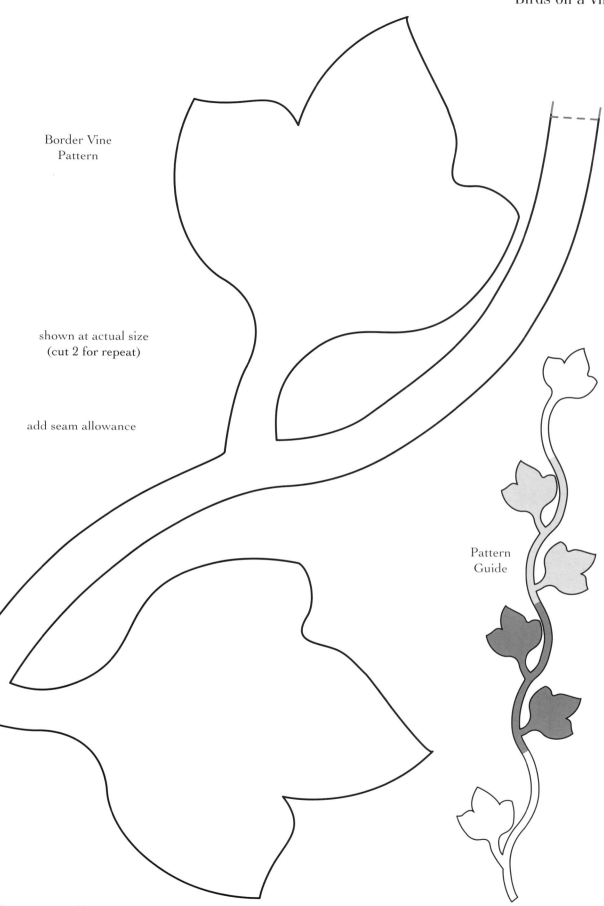

Border Vine
Pattern

shown at actual size
(cut 2 for repeat)

add seam allowance

Pattern
Guide

BEST OF FOUR BLOCKS...AND MORE *Linda Giesler Carlson*

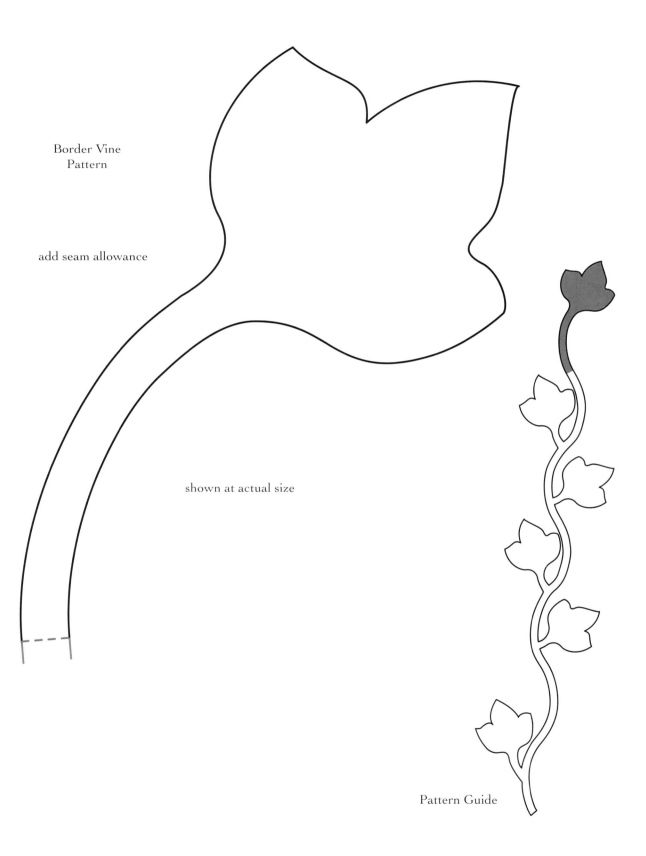

Border Vine
Pattern

add seam allowance

shown at actual size

Pattern Guide

Poinsettia

Feathered Star

POINSETTIA FEATHERED STAR, 82" x 82", 1996. Made by the author. Quick and easy machine-piecing methods provide a simple, yet intricate-looking Feathered Star block. Because the four blocks are set on point, a fifth block is created in the center. By changing its coloration, the center block becomes the focal point of the quilt. Beaded berries add a special holiday feel.

Fabric Requirements

The quilt in the photo on page 43 has larger blocks than the pattern; therefore, fewer half-square triangle units are necessary for this pattern.

If preferred, a third color may be used for the large center square. Make sure the color contrasts with the poinsettia scherenschnitte so it will be seen.

3½ yards white
1¾ yards red
1 yard green
⅞ yard total assorted prints for nine poinsettias

3½ yards print for borders and 2¼" x 336" (eight strips 2¼" x 44") bias binding
Red or yellow scraps for berries

Supplies

Basic sewing kit, page 21
4 large zipper plastic bags
Scrap template plastic and paper
24" or longer rotary ruler
Sparkling beads
6" square or larger rotary ruler with 45-degree diagonal (optional)
Batting for 81½" square
Backing for 81½" square

Cutting Instructions

Use your favorite half-square triangle method for cutting the red and white C triangles.

(4) red 8½" squares for A
(1) green 8½" square for A
(16) red 4⅞" squares, cut once diagonally, for B
(4) green 4⅞" squares, cut once diagonally, for B
(56) red 1⅞" squares, cut once diagonally, for C
(14) green 1⅞" squares, cut once diagonally, for C
(90) white 1⅞" squares, cut once diagonally, for C
(72) red 2" squares, cut once diagonally, for D
(18) green 2" squares, cut once diagonally, for D
(110) white 2" squares, cut once diagonally, for D
(16) red E and (16) red Er, template on page 46
(4) green E and (4) green Er, template
(5) white 11¼" squares, cut twice diagonally, for F
(20) white 6⅛" squares for G
(2) white 15⅞" squares, cut once diagonally, for the corner triangles
(1) white 31¼" square, cut twice diagonally, for setting triangles
(9) assorted green 10" squares for poinsettia scherenschnitte
(70) red 2⅞" squares, cut once diagonally, for sawtooth border

(70) green 2⅞" squares, cut once diagonally, for sawtooth border
(2) print 9½" x 64" strips for top and bottom borders
(2) print 9½" x 82" strips for side borders

Half-Square Triangle Assembly

Make sure you have an accurate ¼" seam allowance on your machine. To check, place a ruler with the ¼" line directly under the needle. A piece of masking tape or moleskin pad on the throat plate beside the ruler is a helpful fabric guide.

1. Label two plastic bags as C and two bags as D to store the different-sized feather units.

2. Make the following half-square triangle units: 112 with the red and white C triangles, 28 with the green and white C triangles, 144 with the red and white D triangles, and 36 with the green and white D triangles.

3. Press the seams on the units closed with an up and down motion to prevent distortion. Then, open the seam and press both the back and the front of the units. The open seams prevent excess bulk when sewing.

Feather Unit Assembly

1. On the leftover white C and D triangles, make a dot in the seam allowance on the middle of the long side. This dot will be matched to the dot on the E/Er pattern piece when the block is joined.

2. Make Unit 1 with nine red and white D half-square triangle units, two white D triangles, two red B triangles, and one white F triangle as shown. Note that the triangle units are sewn to F with partial seams to facilitate joining units 1 and 2. Make 16 of the red and white Unit 1.

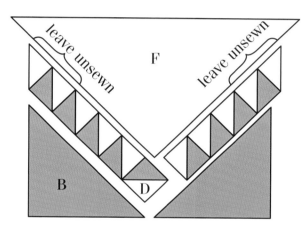

3. Make four of Unit 1 as before, substituting red with green for the half-square triangle units and B triangles.

4. Make Unit 2 with seven red and white C half-square triangle units, two white C triangles, one red E piece, one red Er piece, and one white G square. Make 16 of the red and white Unit 2.

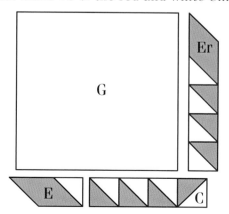

5. Make Unit 2 as before, substituting red with green for the half-square triangle units and E and Er pieces.

Block Assembly

1. For color placement of the units in the blocks, refer to the quilt photo on page 43. Refer to the block assembly diagram, page 47, and sew Unit 1 to each side of an A square to form the middle row of the block.

2. For the top and bottom rows, join Unit 2 to each side of Unit 1, sewing the long seam first. Sew the remaining partial seams of Unit 1 to join the units, matching the dots on the E/Er pattern pieces to the D triangles.

3. Join the three rows, sewing the long seams between the rows first. Then, sew the remaining partial seams of Unit 1 to complete the block.

Poinsettia Scherenschnitte

1. Trace the Poinsettia pattern on template plastic and cut out. Fold a 10" square in half, wrong sides together, then in half again, marking the center fold. Place the template on the fabric, matching fold lines and trace. Holding the folded fabric, cut out all four layers 1/8" away from solid lines. Do not cut on the folds. Repeat with the remaining 10" squares.

2. Center the patterns on the Feathered Star blocks and needle-turn appliqué with an 1/8" seam allowance.

3. To make beaded berries, follow the directions in BIRDS ON A VINE, page 37. Make a cluster of four or a wreath of seven berries for each of the nine poinsettia scherenschnitte.

Quilt Top Assembly

1. Refer to the quilt assembly diagram, page 47, and join the Feathered Star blocks, corner triangles,

and setting triangles in diagonal rows as shown. Trim the side and corner triangles to size, leaving a ¼" seam allowance, after adding them to the blocks.

2. For the sawtooth border, make 140 half-square triangle units with the red and green border triangles. Press the seam allowances open as before. Right sides together, sew two sets of 34 and two sets of 36 units. Sew the shorter sets to top and bottom of quilt. Press seam allowances toward the quilt. Sew the remaining sets to the sides of the quilt. Press.

3. Sew the 64" borders to the top and bottom of quilt. Press seam allowance toward outer border. Sew the 82" borders to sides of quilt. Press seam allowances.

Finishing

1. Mark quilt as desired.

2. Layer backing, batting, and top. Baste and quilt.

3. Apply binding following the general directions, page 23.

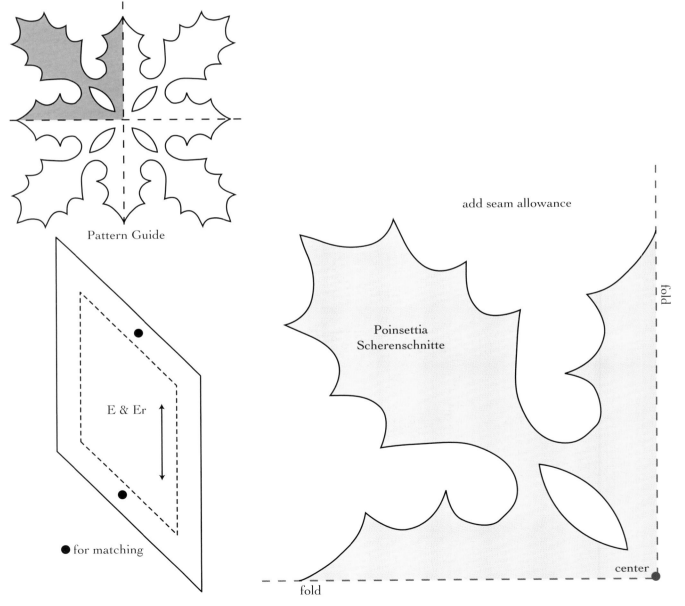

Pattern Guide

E & Er

● for matching

Poinsettia Scherenschnitte

add seam allowance

fold

fold

center

Block Assembly

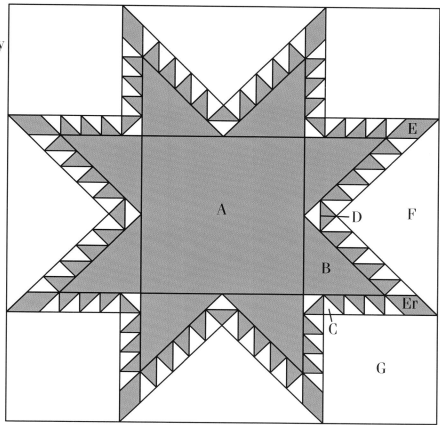

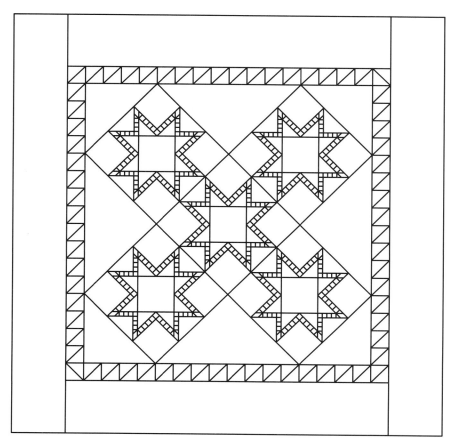

Quilt Assembly

Prince of Wales Feathers and Crown, 88" x 88", 1994. Made by the author. This quilt was inspired by the Aumiller County, Pennsylvania, Red and Gray Prince's Feather quilt found by the Oral Traditions Project.

Fabric Requirements

4 yards background fabric

4½ yards for borders and binding

1 yard for feathers

2 yards primary geese color for sashing, center, and inner sawtooth borders

1¾ yards secondary geese color for sashing and sawtooth background inner borders

¼ yard for (4) stars

¾ yard for crown

(16) 4" x 3" scraps for leaves

Acrylic yarn for trapunto stems on feathers, leaves, and crown; yarn needle (optional)

Supplies

1 large sheet template plastic or freezer paper

Fabric scissors

Template cutting scissors

Appliqué needle

Threads to match fabrics

Fabric pencil

Batting and backing for 88" square

Make freezer-paper or plastic templates and trace around them on the right side of the fabric for appliquéing. Add ⅛" seam allowance to fabric pieces when cutting.

Cutting Instructions

Instructions on the pattern pieces are for one block, unless otherwise noted.

(4) 28½" background squares

(2) 12½" x 88½" side borders

(2) 12½" x 64½" top and bottom borders

(4) pieces A for crown

(4) pieces B for star; mark top of star on template

(16) pieces C for leaves

(12) pieces D for feathers

Binding strips to equal 2¼" x 365"

Block Assembly

1. Position and pin crown (A) in the bottom right corner of the background block about 1" inside the bottom and side edges.

2. Position and pin star (B) so that the bottom point fits under the top left corner of the crown.

3. Pin leaves (C) to four star points as shown.

4. Position and pin three feathers (D) on remaining star points.

5. Appliqué feathers first by needle-turning edges under so that marking lines do not show. Clip inner and outer curves where necessary, cutting through the marking lines. This ensures smooth feather edges as well as narrow spacing between feathers. *Option: Stitch ¼" wide channels for stems on the feathers and leaves. Stitch circular channels to resemble jewels on the crown. Insert yarn from the back.*

6. Appliqué star. Points should just touch the bottom spines of the feathers, not overlap. Cut into right angles between points to ensure a smooth turn under. Turn under the raw edge on the pencil line. Sew up to pencil line star tip and take two stitches to hold it down while you needle-turn the folded raw edge underneath the star point and back toward the sewn edge. Once the raw edge is stuffed under and away from

clip inner corner

two stitches

the star point, continue to needle-turn under the star sides. Take two appliqué stitches in the inner angles to keep the raw edge from raveling.

7. Appliqué leaves, starting on a side, at least 1" away from the bottom of the leaf. As you work toward the star point, needle-turn the leaf edge in the same manner as the star point. Allow the bottom leaf point to barely touch the star point.

8. Appliqué the edges of the crown, allowing the top left section to touch the bottom point with a slight overlap. Clip the curves and inner angles as necessary.

Sashing Assembly

1. You will need 56 finished Flying Geese squares. Cut (14) 5¼" squares from geese fabric (white in photo), and (28) 2⅞" squares background fabric (dark purple in photo). Follow the directions for Flying Geese Squares, page 22.

2. Join 14 Flying Geese units for each of the four sashes. Noting geese and block directions in the photo, sew a sashing vertically between two blocks. Repeat for the remaining two blocks.

3. The center of the quilt is two Flying Geese in the reverse coloration from the sashing. Cut (1) 5¼" square background color for the center two geese. Cut (3) 2⅞" squares of the geese color that will now be the background. Sew together to yield two geese units.

4. Add one reverse coloration unit to the right end of a 14 geese sashing flying west. Sew the other reverse geese unit to the left end of a 14 geese sashing flying east.

5. Join the west geese units to the east geese units with the two reverse coloration geese units forming an on-point square in the center.

6. Match and pin center sashes to the top two blocks and sew together.

7. Repeat matching and pinning of the center sashes to the bottom two blocks.

Sawtooth Inner Borders

1. Follow the directions for making 124 sawtooth squares, page 21, using (2) 42" x 16" pieces of the main sawtooth color and its background color (white and dark purple in the photo).

2. On the wrong side of the lightest fabric, draw a grid of (62) 2⅞" squares. Continue according to directions.

3. See quilt photo. Above the top two blocks, notice how the sawtooth border changes directions in the center. Join (15) sawtooth squares one way, then make a row of (15) in the opposite direction. Sew these rows together to make a (30) sawtooth border.

4. Match and pin to Flying Geese sashing and ends. Sew together. Repeat steps 3 and 4 for the bottom two blocks.

5. The side sawtooth borders have 32 units joined, reversing the sawtooth direction in the center as before, as well as turning both end units a quarter turn. See quilt photo. Match, pin, and sew as in Step 4.

Finishing

1. Layer backing, batting, and quilt top.

2. Baste and quilt as desired.

3. Apply binding following general directions, page 23.

A

A
Crown
(cut 1)

Pattern Guide

reverse pattern here for other side

add seam allowance

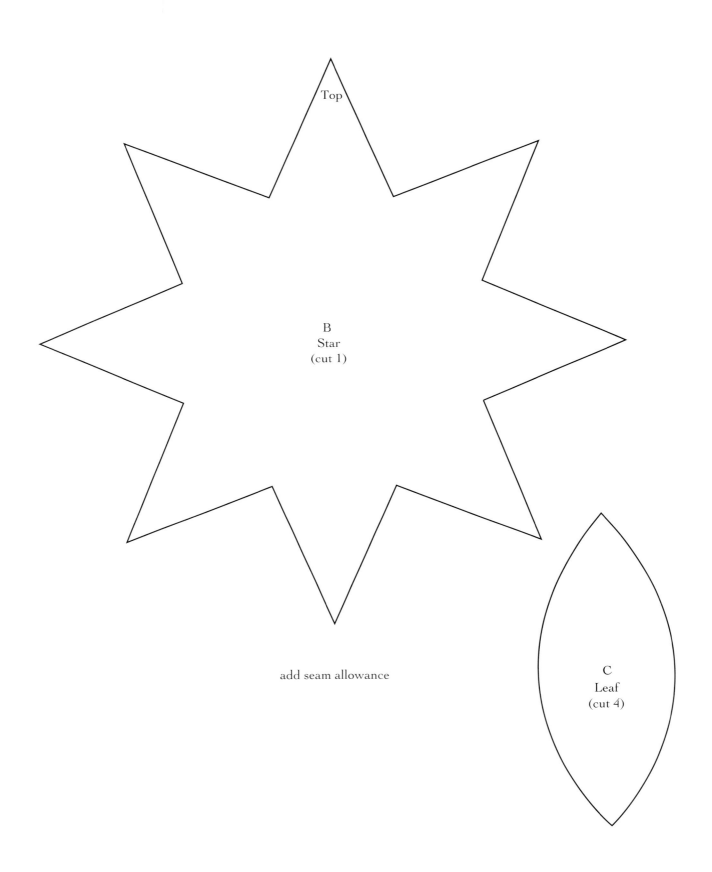

Top

B
Star
(cut 1)

add seam allowance

C
Leaf
(cut 4)

BEST OF FOUR BLOCKS…AND MORE *Linda Giesler Carlson*

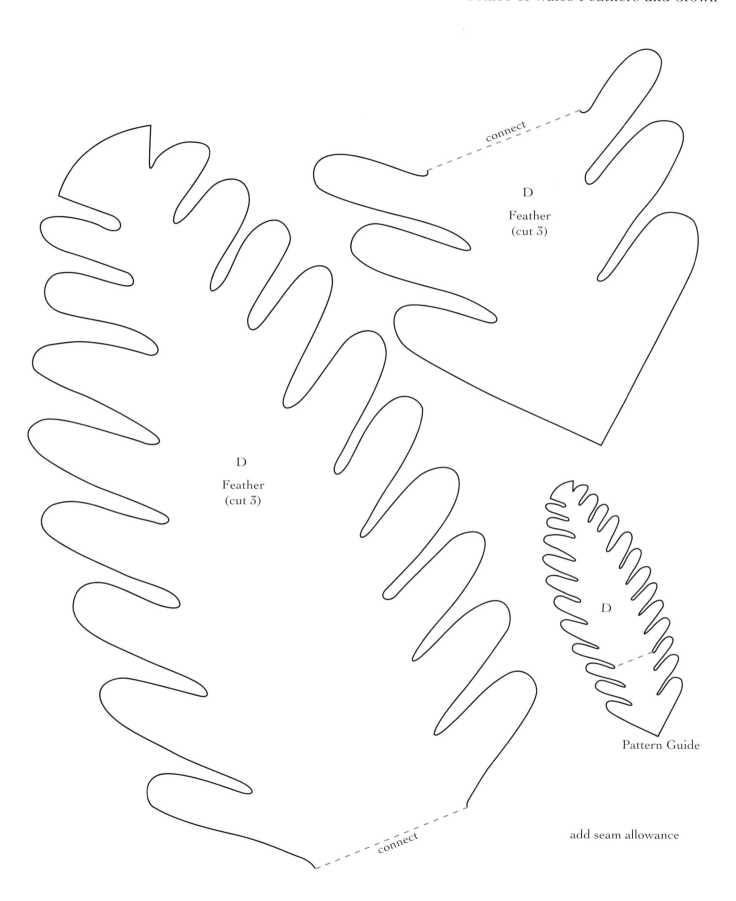

connect

D
Feather
(cut 3)

D
Feather
(cut 3)

D

connect

Pattern Guide

add seam allowance

COXCOMB CROSSING, 112" x 112", 1994. Made by the author. This large block was inspired by an antique multi-block quilt, ca. 1860–1875, owned by the Audrain County Historical Society Museum in Mexico, Missouri. It was donated by Miss Virginia Botts, whose ancestors came from Kentucky. A very similar quilt was found by the Kentucky Quilt Project. I have named it COXCOMB CROSSING, as it has previously been called "Unknown" by Barbara Brackman, author of *Encyclopedia of Appliqué.*

Fabric Requirements

11¾ yards white for blocks and borders

2 yards green

3 yards red

2½ yards pink

½ yard yellow

2¼ yards floral print

⅛ yard dark green

¾ yard binding

Supplies

Basic sewing kit, page 21

Compass

Batting and backing for 112" square

Cutting Instructions

Instructions on the pattern pieces are for one block, unless otherwise noted.

(4) 42½" squares for blocks

(2) 14½" x 84½" borders

(2) 14½" x 112½" borders

(4) yellow A

(16) red B

(32) green and (32) pink C

(32) green and (32) pink Cr

(16) green D

(16) green E

(16) yellow F

(80) pink and (18) red G

(64) red and (18) pink H

(80) red and (18) pink I

(16) white J and (16) white Jr

(16) green K and (16) green Kr

(16) white L and (16) white Lr

(16) green M and (16) green Mr

(16) white N and (16) white Nr

(16) white O

(44) floral P

(12) dark green Q

(4) pink and (4) red R

(4) red S

(4) floral T

(4) green and (4) dark green U

(1) floral 6" circle (Center Appliqué, Step 1, page 58)

Make 2¼" x 455" (eleven 2¼" x 44" strips) binding

Trace all templates on the wrong side of the fabric, except for P through U. Add a ¼" seam allowance to all pieces.

Join five of the P pieces end to end eight times to make the border appliqués.

Block Assembly

Crossing Section

1. Sew the crossing section of the block. Piece Unit 1 by sewing a B piece to each side of an A piece.

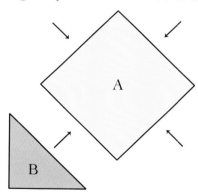

2. Piece eight sets of one green C and one pink C triangle to form individual rectangles. Repeat to make eight sets of green and pink Cr triangles.

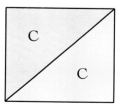
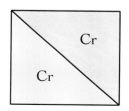

3. Piece Unit 2 by sewing two rectangles, short ends together. Keep the C rectangles separate from the Cr rectangles.

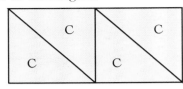

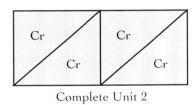

Complete Unit 2

4. Sew D stem to a pair of C rectangles. Repeat with the remaining three pairs of C rectangles.

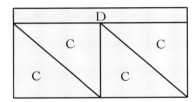

5. Sew Cr rectangle pairs to the other side of the D stem units.

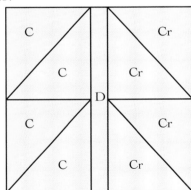

6. For the top row of the inner crossing block, sew an O piece to each side of a pieced Unit 2, noting the unit's direction.

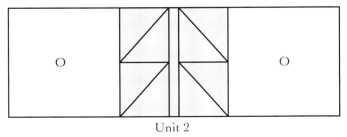

Unit 2

7. To complete the middle row, sew Unit 2 to each side of Unit 1, noting opposing directions of each Unit 2.

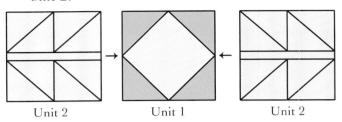

Unit 2   Unit 1   Unit 2

8. Sew the bottom row the same as the top row, but reverse the direction of Unit 2.

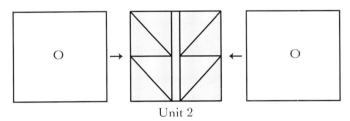

Unit 2

9. Join the top row to the middle row, butting seam allowances of units. Then add to bottom row in same manner. Set this inner crossing section aside.

Coxcomb Section

10. To piece the coxcomb sections, separate fabric pieces and the reverse pieces. For the leaf section, Unit 3, sew J to K, then add L. Repeat for Jr, Kr, and Lr. Continue in same manner for the three remaining flowers.

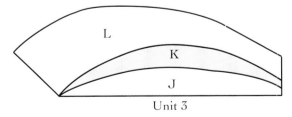

Unit 3

11. Sew short stem E to J-K-L, then join the Jr, Kr, Lr section. Repeat for the other flowers.

Complete Unit 3

12. Piece F must be set into Unit 3 by first sewing the flat bottom to the top of E. Attach F's bias

sides to L by starting at the corners of E and sewing toward the top arch of F.

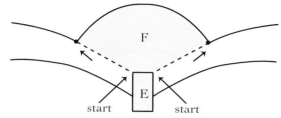

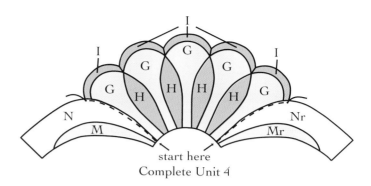

start here
Complete Unit 4

13. Sew five I pieces to five G pieces for each of the four flowers. *Hint: Pin the beginning and end of pieces, then in the middle, distributing fullness evenly. Clip only if necessary to ease curve.* Add H to one side of G-I section; then attach another G-I section to the H just sewn. Sew the two I's from their inner corners outward.

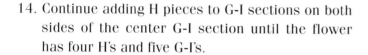

Unit 4

14. Continue adding H pieces to G-I sections on both sides of the center G-I section until the flower has four H's and five G-I's.

15. Sew M to N. Repeat for Mr and Nr and remaining three flowers.

16. Attach M-N and Mr-Nr sections to the ends of the coxcombs, starting at bottom of first and last G pieces and sewing outward to complete Unit 4.

17. Sew Unit 3 to Unit 4. Pin and sew the yellow center F first. Starting where the inner edge of Lr meets Mr, pin the F piece to Unit 4, ending with M being even with the curved edge of F. Ease, if necessary, and sew. Sew remaining parts of units 3 and 4 by starting at outer corner of F, pinning L to M and sewing outward. Repeat at the beginning corner of F for attaching Lr to Mr. Complete remaining flowers in the same manner.

18. Sew bottom of each Unit 3 to four sides of inner crossing. Attach diagonal edges of L-M-N to adjacent Coxcomb by starting at inner corner of block and sewing outward. Repeat for all corners. Center and pin the block onto 42½" background. Turn fabric under on pencil lines of I, N, and Nr pieces and appliqué all edges. Carefully cut back of block ¼" to ½" away from the appliqué stitching. Join the four blocks. See illustration on page 58.

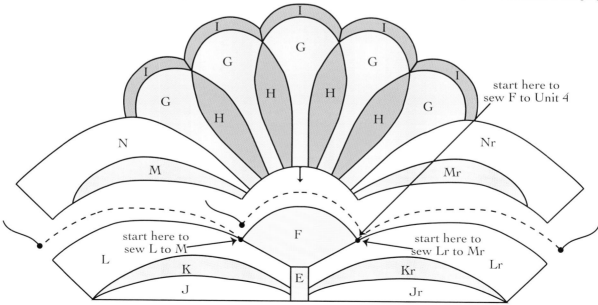

start here to
sew F to Unit 4

start here to
sew L to M

start here to
sew Lr to Mr

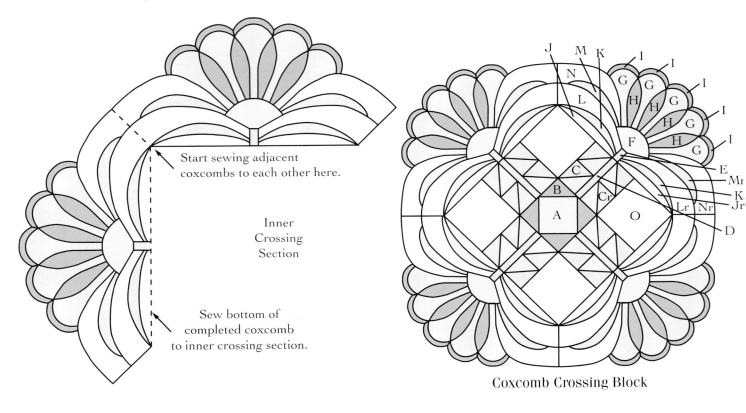

Start sewing adjacent coxcombs to each other here.

Inner Crossing Section

Sew bottom of completed coxcomb to inner crossing section.

Coxcomb Crossing Block

Center Appliqué

1. Draw a circle with the compass, 5½" in diameter on the right side of the floral fabric. This will be the sewing line. Enlarge the compass to 6" and make another circle around the first. This gives an accurate ¼" seam allowance for appliquéing over the bases of the G-H-I units.

2. Match and pin I to G as in Step 13, page 57. Distribute the fullness evenly. Clip only if necessary to ease curve. Sew. Repeat for all 18 units.

3. Add H to one side of the G-I unit. Attach another G-I unit to the first H. Sew both I pieces from the inner corner outward.

4. Continue adding H pieces to the other G-I units. Join each I piece until all 18 form a circle.

5. Flatten the circle on an ironing board. Iron on a low setting, barely pressing, if necessary. Hot ironing could stretch the motif.

6. Center the 5½" circle over the G-H-I unit. Needle-turn the edges under and appliqué in place.

7. Place the completed motif over the quilt center. Pin and needle-turn appliqué in place, leaving ½" to ¾" open over each seam line for the branches to be inserted.

8. Reverse appliqué a scrap piece of material under four Q pieces. Refer to the Center Appliqué diagram, page 59, and pin the four P pieces in each of the center motif openings.

9. Pin and appliqué the complete Q pieces under the branches as shown. Place two R pieces, one red and one pink, beside Q and appliqué. Appliqué the branch in place. Repeat for the remaining branches.

Borders

The borders should be appliquéd before being attached to the quilt top.

1. Find the center of each border by folding horizontally and vertically. Iron lightly.

2. Refer to the Border Appliqué diagram and appliqué the curved top edge of T onto S. Baste the bottom of T to S. Repeat for the remaining units.

3. Center and pin the end petals of the T-S unit over the center of each border. To make a long branch, pin five P pieces on the border's vertical pressed line with their ends tucked under the T-S side petals. Appliqué the branch in place, leaving the outer end open.

4. Appliqué T-S in place except for the bottom edges. Pin two U pieces, a green and a dark green, to bottom edge of T-S unit. Appliqué in place. Repeat for remaining borders.

5. Center and pin the 14½" x 84½" border to the top of the quilt. Sew. Repeat for bottom border. Center and sew each 14½" x 112½" side border.

Finishing

1. Layer backing, batting, and quilt top.

2. Baste and quilt as desired.

3. Apply binding following general directions, page 23.

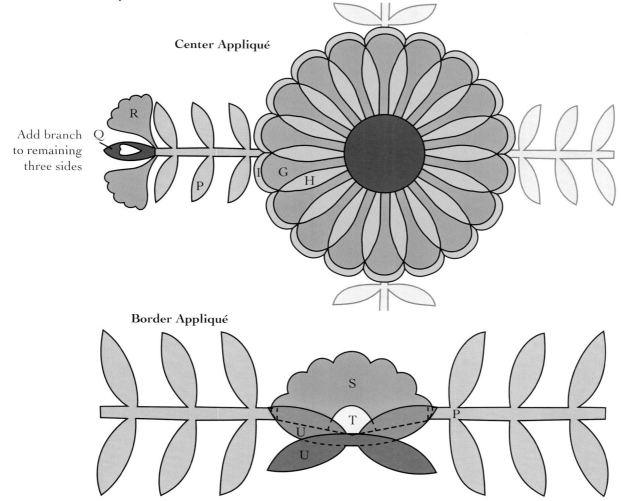

Center Appliqué

Add branch to remaining three sides

Border Appliqué

Coxcomb Crossing

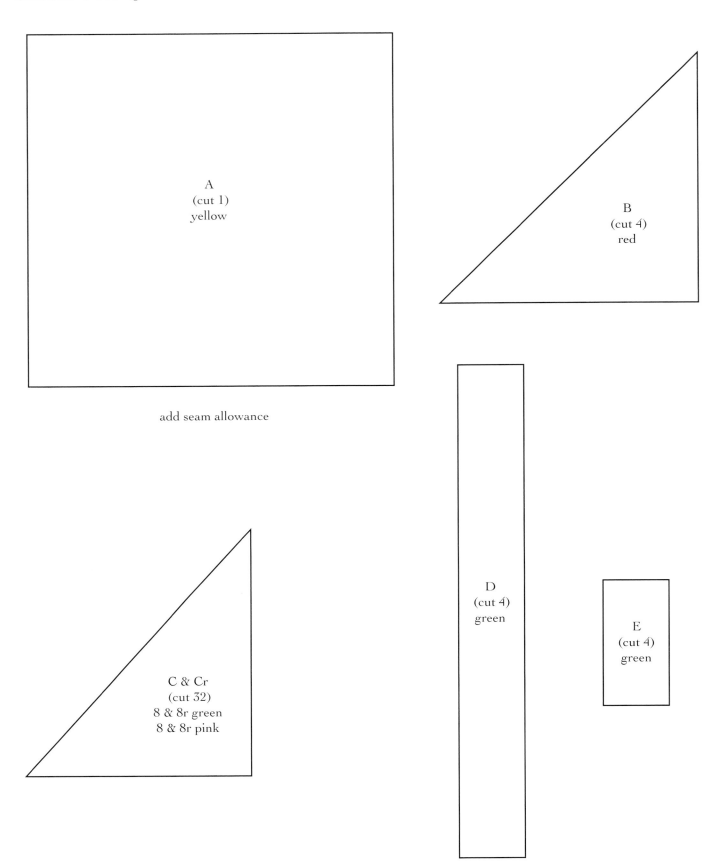

A
(cut 1)
yellow

add seam allowance

B
(cut 4)
red

D
(cut 4)
green

E
(cut 4)
green

C & Cr
(cut 32)
8 & 8r green
8 & 8r pink

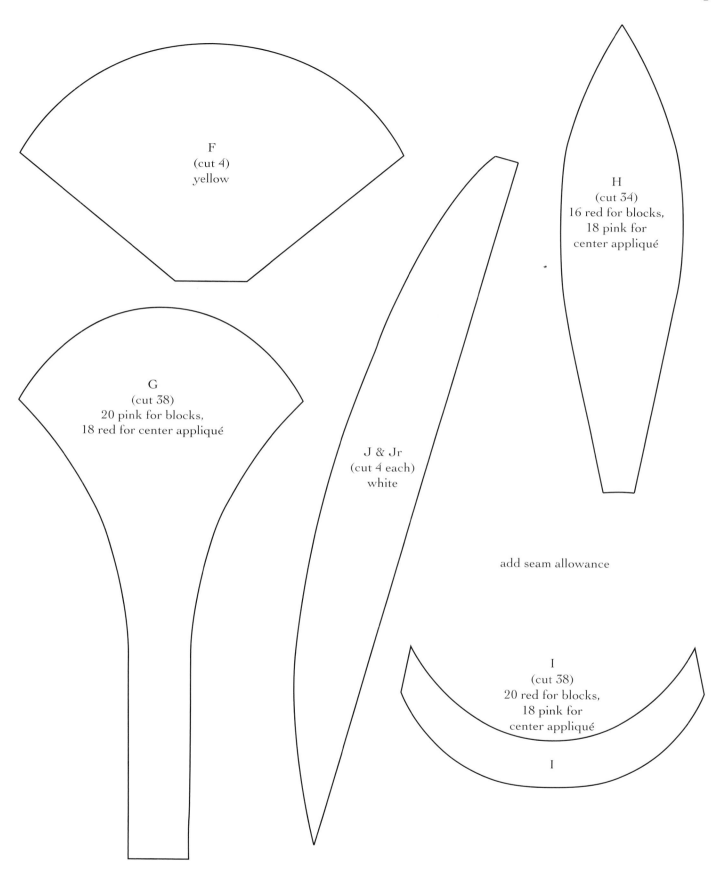

F
(cut 4)
yellow

H
(cut 34)
16 red for blocks,
18 pink for
center appliqué

G
(cut 38)
20 pink for blocks,
18 red for center appliqué

J & Jr
(cut 4 each)
white

add seam allowance

I
(cut 38)
20 red for blocks,
18 pink for
center appliqué

I

Coxcomb Crossing

add seam allowance

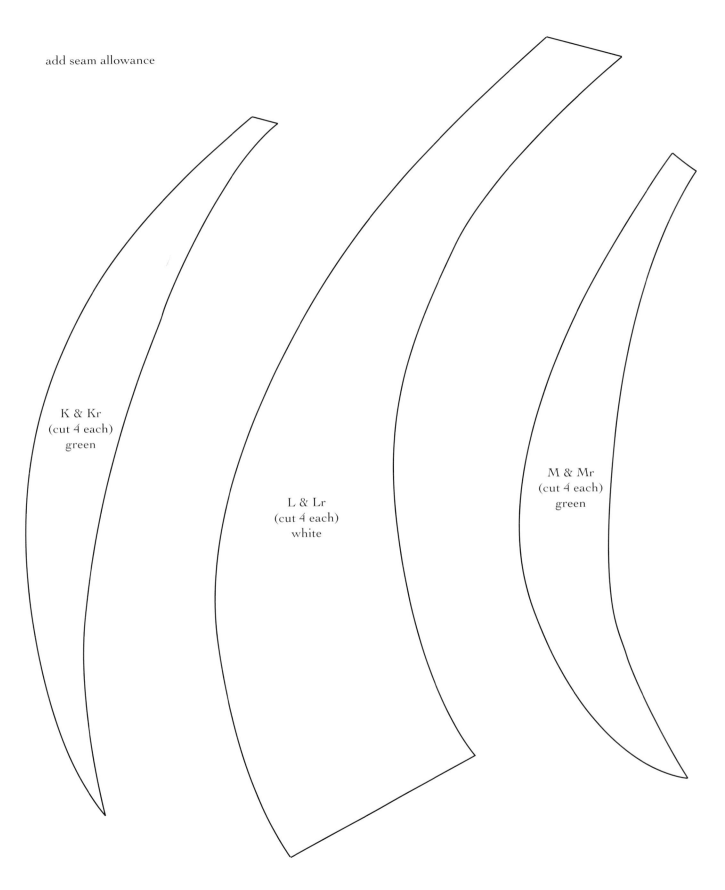

K & Kr
(cut 4 each)
green

L & Lr
(cut 4 each)
white

M & Mr
(cut 4 each)
green

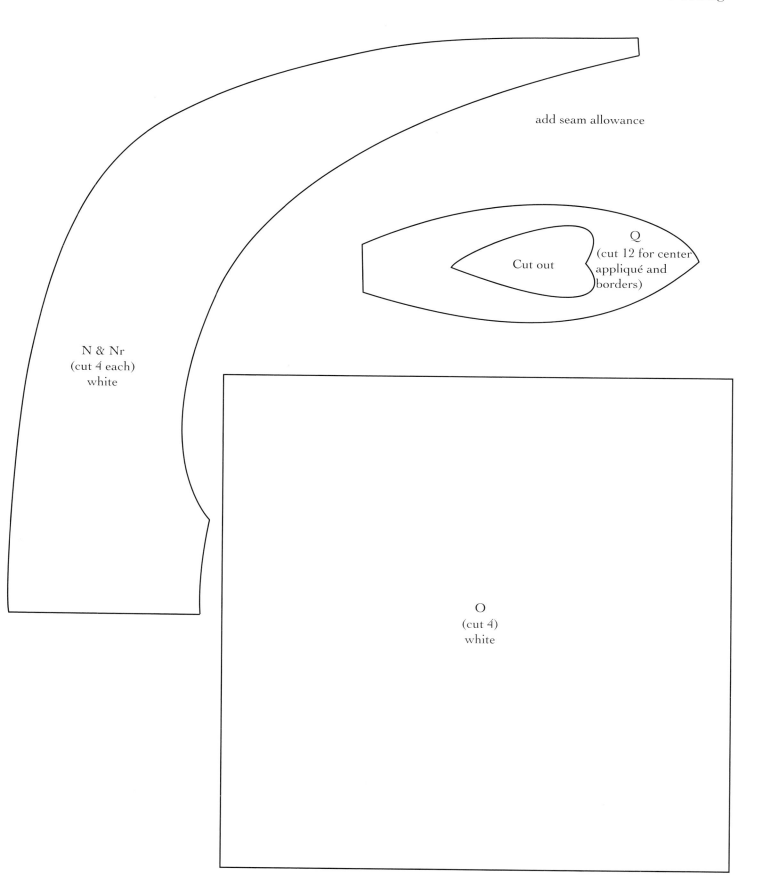

add seam allowance

Q
(cut 12 for center
appliqué and
borders)

Cut out

N & Nr
(cut 4 each)
white

O
(cut 4)
white

P
(cut 44 for center and
border appliqué)

add seam allowance

U
(cut 4 green and
4 dark green
for border appliqué)

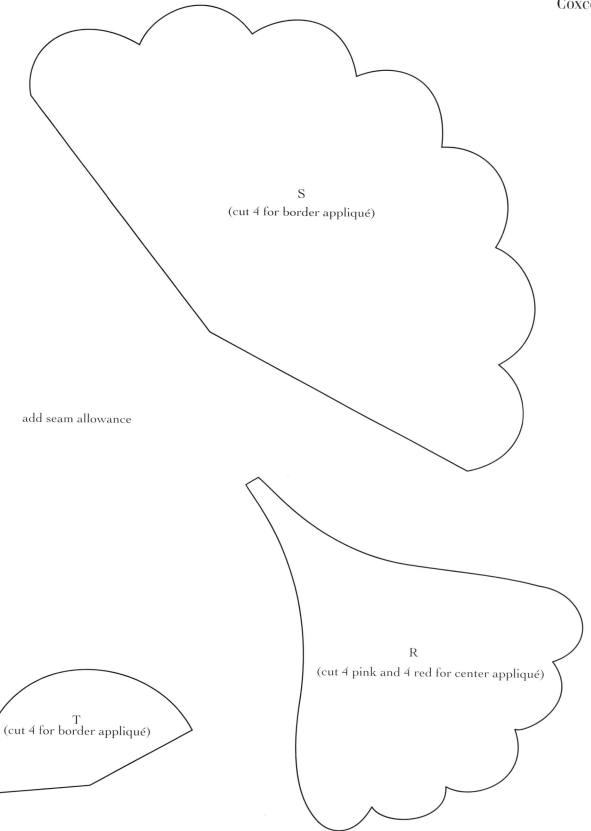

S
(cut 4 for border appliqué)

add seam allowance

R
(cut 4 pink and 4 red for center appliqué)

T
(cut 4 for border appliqué)

Whig-Harrison

Rose Quilt

WHIG-HARRISON ROSE, 90" x 90", 1994. Made by the author. Traditional colors of red, gold, and green are used in the flowers of this quilt. The rose centers are bordered with rosebuds in an asymmetrical design.

Fabric Requirements

4 yards background color
½ yard yellow
½ yard red
1 yard dark red
2 yards dark green
½ yard medium green print
3½ yards border and binding fabric
5" square for center appliqué center
6" square for center appliqué middle petals
8" square for center appliqué outer petals

Supplies

Basic sewing kit, page 21
Batting for 90" square
Backing for 90" square
1 large sheet template
Plastic or freezer paper

Cutting Instructions

Instructions on the pattern pieces are for one block, unless otherwise noted.

(4) 35½" blocks of background fabric
(2) 10½" x 70½" top and bottom borders of print
(2) 10½" x 90½" side borders of print
Make 2¼" x 365" (nine 2¼" x 44" strips) binding
(4) red A
(36) dark red B
(36) yellow C
(16) green print D
(16) dark green E
(16) red F
(16) dark red G
(8) yellow H and (8) yellow Hr
(56) red H and (40) red Hr
(48) dark green I and (48) dark green Ir
(1) each of J, K, and L

Trace all templates on right side of fabric, except B. Trace B on wrong side of red because the short, straight sides will be pieced. Add an ⅛" seam allowance on all pieces.

Block Assembly

1. Piece short, straight sides of B pieces together to form a circle. Finger press under curved edges on pencil lines.

2. Fold the background block in half twice to find the center. Finger press the center and open.

3. Position the B circle in the center and pin. Lay A over raw edges of inner B circle. Needle-turn the edges of A and appliqué.

4. Finger press the outer curved edge of the C pieces on the pencil line. Insert C's between B's and temporarily pin in place.

5. Insert, position, and pin D leaves under Harrison Rose. Insert, position, and pin four E rose branches under Harrison Rose.

6. Appliqué the B pieces over the C pieces, leaves, and rose branches. Appliqué C pieces over leaves and rose branches.

7. Finish sewing leaves and branches, inserting four H buds where necessary.

8. Position and appliqué red F pieces to G pieces. Position each F-G at the ends of the rose branches and appliqué. *Option: The number of bud stems can vary.*

9. Surround the Whig-Harrison Rose with a circle of buds. Trace the bud stem from the E rose

branch onto the top of the dark green fabric. Using red, pink, and yellow, make buds with pattern piece H on the right side of the fabrics. Only trace four yellow buds, which should be placed under the bud stems pointing toward the center Harrison Rose.

10. Lay the bud stems around the floral "X" with the stems under the buds. Adjust so that the design is pleasing to the eye, and pin. Insert the buds, alternating red and pink, and appliqué all pieces in place. Join the four blocks.

Center Appliqué

1. Trace each pattern (J, K, L) individually onto freezer paper. Trace on the right side of the fabric. Cut out with an ⅛" seam allowance.

2. Position J on K. Pin and needle-turn the seam allowance and appliqué.

3. Pin the J-K unit on L and appliqué.

4. Center the J-K-L unit over the center and appliqué.

Borders

1. Fold and finger press the center of the 10½" x 70½" borders. Match the top border and pin outward from the center seam. Sew.

2. Repeat for the bottom border.

3. Find the center of the 10½" x 90½" side borders. Match and pin each from the center seam outward. Sew.

Finishing

1. Mark the four blocks first with the fan quilting motif. Cover the entire quilt except for the center motif.

2. Leave a ¼" margin around the center motif. Mark the center motif with the quilting lines that are shown with the pattern on page 70.

3. Layer the backing, batting, and top. Baste and quilt.

4. Apply binding following general directions, page 23.

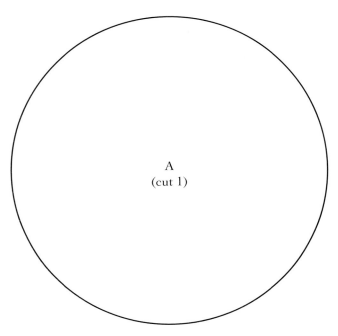

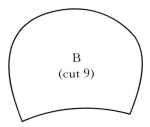

add seam allowance

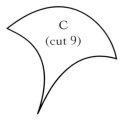

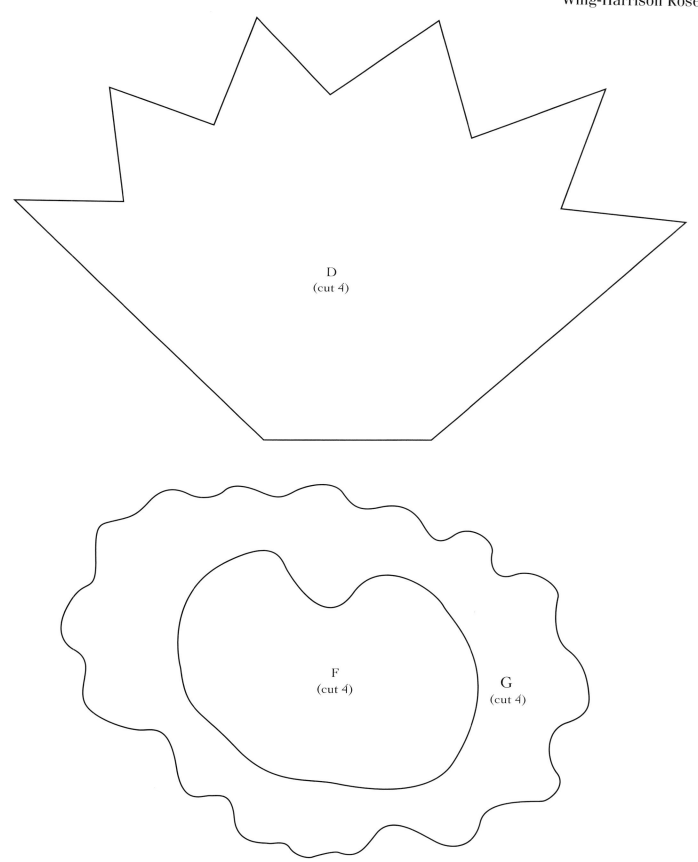

D
(cut 4)

F
(cut 4)

G
(cut 4)

Fan Quilting Design
(enlarge to 5")

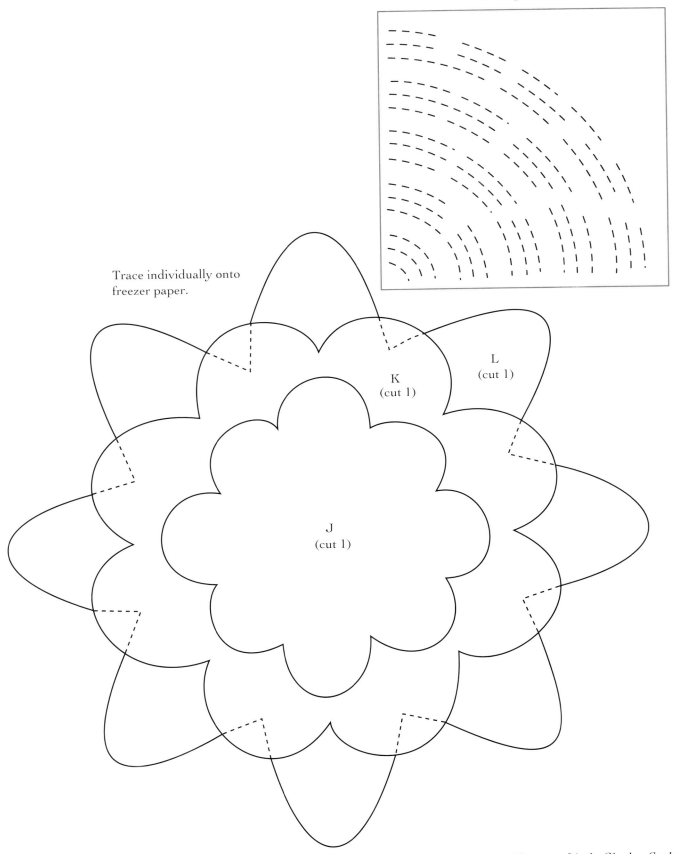

Trace individually onto
freezer paper.

K
(cut 1)

L
(cut 1)

J
(cut 1)

BEST OF FOUR BLOCKS...AND MORE *Linda Giesler Carlson*

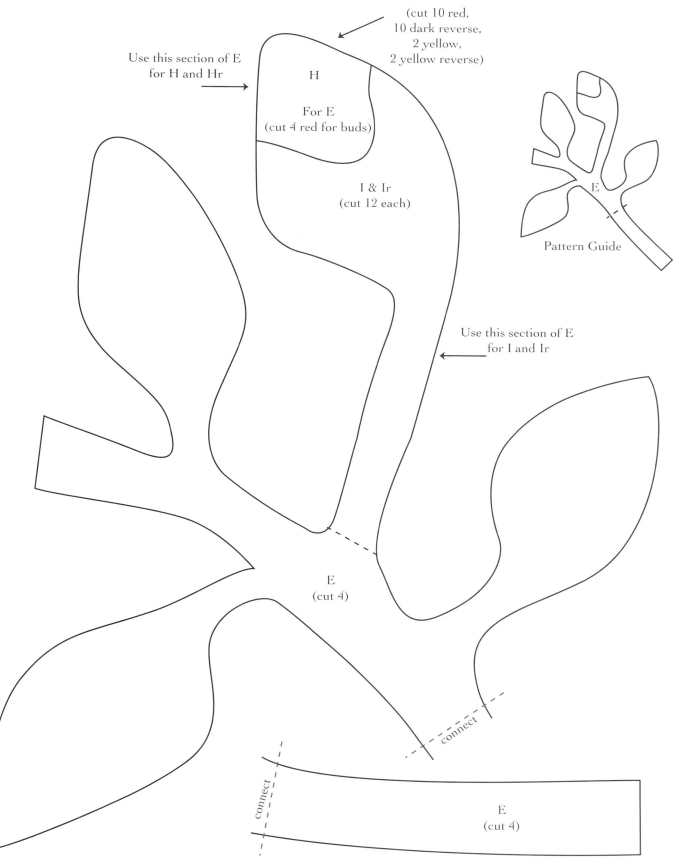

(cut 10 red,
10 dark reverse,
2 yellow,
2 yellow reverse)

Use this section of E
for H and Hr

H

For E
(cut 4 red for buds)

I & Ir
(cut 12 each)

E

Pattern Guide

Use this section of E
for I and Ir

E
(cut 4)

connect

connect

E
(cut 4)

PRINCESS FEATHER, 102" x 102", 1992. Made by the author and quilted by Katie Borntreger, Verona, Missouri. Photo by Richard Walker.

BEST OF FOUR BLOCKS...AND MORE *Linda Giesler Carlson*

Fabric Requirements

5 yards for blocks and feathers in the border

5 yards for borders

3 yards of first feather color, large stars, and inner dogtooth border

2 yards of second feather color and medium stars

4 yards of third color for small accent stars, outer dogtooth border, piping, and binding

7¾ yards of ¼" cording

Supplies

2 large sheets template plastic or freezer paper

Fabric scissors and template cutting scissors

Appliqué needles

Threads to match fabrics

Fabric pencil and chalk pencil

Backing and batting for 108" square

Make templates and trace on right side of fabric for appliquéing. Add seam allowance to fabric pieces.

Cutting Instructions

(4) 34½" blocks of background color

(16) feathers of the first color

(16) feathers of the second color

(4) large stars of the first color*

(5) medium stars of the second color

(5) small stars of the third color

(2) borders 17½" x 102½"

(2) borders 17½" x 68½"

(4) 10" x 40" strips of background color for reverse appliqué in borders

(4) 2½" x 70" strips of first color for inner dogtooth border

(4) 2½" x 103" strips of third color for outer dogtooth border

Make 2½" x 412" (ten 2½" x 44" strips) binding

Make 11½ yards of 1" bias from third color to cover piping cord around outer edges of four sewn blocks

*Add ½" turn-under allowance when cutting out circle inside star instead of the usual ¼".

Block Assembly

Instructions are for one block. Repeat process for remaining three blocks. Use needle-turn appliqué technique.

1. Find center of block by folding in half. Finger press. Fold in half again in opposite direction. Finger press. Open block and fold diagonally. Finger press. Repeat in opposite diagonal direction. Open block.

2. Position large star in center with a tip pointing to the top of the block. Pin. (It will be appliquéd later.)

3. Position and pin medium-sized star within the large star, making sure a tip also points directly to the top of the block.

4. Turn under and pin seam allowance of large star center circle. Clip where necessary. Adjust this seam allowance so that when the medium-sized star is sewn, its points will just touch the edge of the circle.

5. Clip inner points on straight edges of stars.

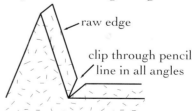

6. Appliqué the medium star in place. Position, pin, and appliqué small star onto medium star. *Option: Appliqué the fifth small star onto the fifth medium star and set aside until all four blocks are joined.*

7. Starting halfway up the star side, turn under the raw edge on the pencil line. Appliqué on pencil line to star point. Take two stitches to hold it down. Needle-turn the folded raw edge underneath the star point and back toward the sewn edge. Continue appliquéing the other side of the star. When you come to the inner angle, take two stitches over the pencil line to anchor any frayed ends. Continue in same manner for rest of the star.

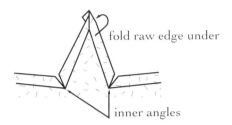

fold raw edge under

inner angles

8. Using only two to three pins, temporarily position the eight alternating-colored feathers between the large star points. Try to space them evenly, and carefully position their curvatures. Fold the spine's seam allowance under the star's inner angles. Pin.

9. Appliqué the large star over the folded feather spines.

10. Complete the pinning of the feathers. Needle-turn the feather edges so that marking lines do not show. Clip inner and outer curves where necessary, cutting through the marked lines, to ensure smooth feather edges as well as narrow spacing between the feathers.

11. Join the four blocks when appliqué is complete.

12. Position and sew fifth appliquéd medium star at center juncture where the four blocks meet.

Piping

1. Fold the 1" wide bias in half, wrong sides together, with one 70" cording tucked inside. Using the zipper foot on your sewing machine, sew ⅛"

away from the cording for the entire length of the bias. *Hint: Lay cording a scant ¼" away from bias raw edge. This will prevent the corner from bunching. Continue in same manner for the remaining three cords.*

← cording

2. Hand or machine sew the piping to the four blocks. Matching raw edges of the piping to the front side of joined blocks, stitch next to the cording inside the first stitching line. Trim any excess piping.

Reverse Appliqué on Borders

1. Fold the borders in half to find the center. Finger press. Center medium-sized star template on fold 4½" from bottom of border. Trace.

2. Trace around feather template with spines tucked under the middle east-west star points. Reverse the template for the left side. Using long stitches, baste the 10" x 40" background strips behind the tracing marks to the back of the border (right side of strip to wrong side of border). Carefully trim inside the tracing lines ¼" for the reverse appliqué seam allowance. Do not cut background strip underneath. Use thread to match border fabric. Clip inner and outer curves as necessary on feathers. Reverse appliqué all four borders.

Appliqué Dogtooth Borders

1. On each 2½" x 70" strip, very lightly with a chalk pencil draw a dotted line 1" from raw edge for the entire length of the strip.

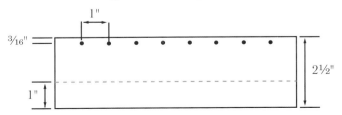

2. On the remaining long raw edge, mark a dot every 1" about ³⁄₁₆" from raw edge.

3. Pin to a 17½" x 68½" border. Starting at right edge of the border, fold under ¼" of the dogtooth border to hide its raw edge. Starting at the first dot, cut a vertical line to the 1" dotted chalk line. Cut every other dot, only a few at a time, being careful to cut only the dogtooth border.

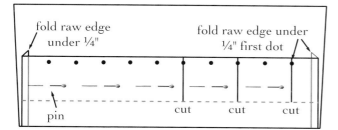

4. Start appliquéing at the folded edge of the dogtooth border. Sew up to the point, treating it the same as the star point. Before sewing the left side of the tooth, fold the triangular raw edge under so that it is about a 60-degree angle. Take two stitches to hold the inner angle securely before folding back the right side of the tooth to continue the process. Don't worry if you have a partial or whole dogtooth at the end of the border. When all four borders are sewn to the blocks, a separate dogtooth can be appliquéd over the corners to make them turn correctly. Our ancestors did this, and we can, too!

5. Turn the border around so that the dogtooth border points to the outer edge of the quilt when the border is sewn to the blocks. Sew border to blocks.

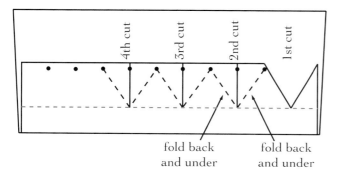

6. Repeat steps 1–5 for the second 17½" x 68½" border.

7. Lay the quilt on the floor or table to determine where to begin pinning the third 2½" x 70" inner dogtooth border.

8. Align 17½" x 102½" border with quilt top. Lay the third inner dogtooth border on the top with the right-hand raw edge turned under ¼". Pin in place. Repeat instructions for the fourth inner dogtooth border.

9. Repeat instructions for the outer 2½" x 103" dogtooth border. The teeth will point to the inner border.

Finishing

1. Mark quilting lines. Layer backing, batting, and quilt top.

2. Baste and quilt as desired.

3. Apply binding following general directions, page 23.

Quilt Assembly

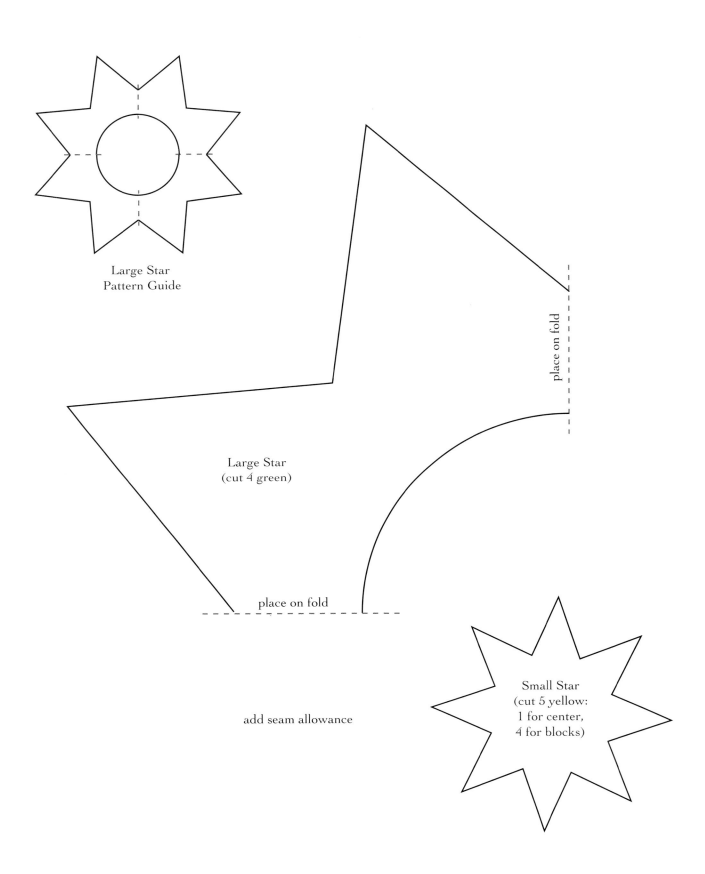

Large Star
Pattern Guide

Large Star
(cut 4 green)

place on fold

place on fold

add seam allowance

Small Star
(cut 5 yellow:
1 for center,
4 for blocks)

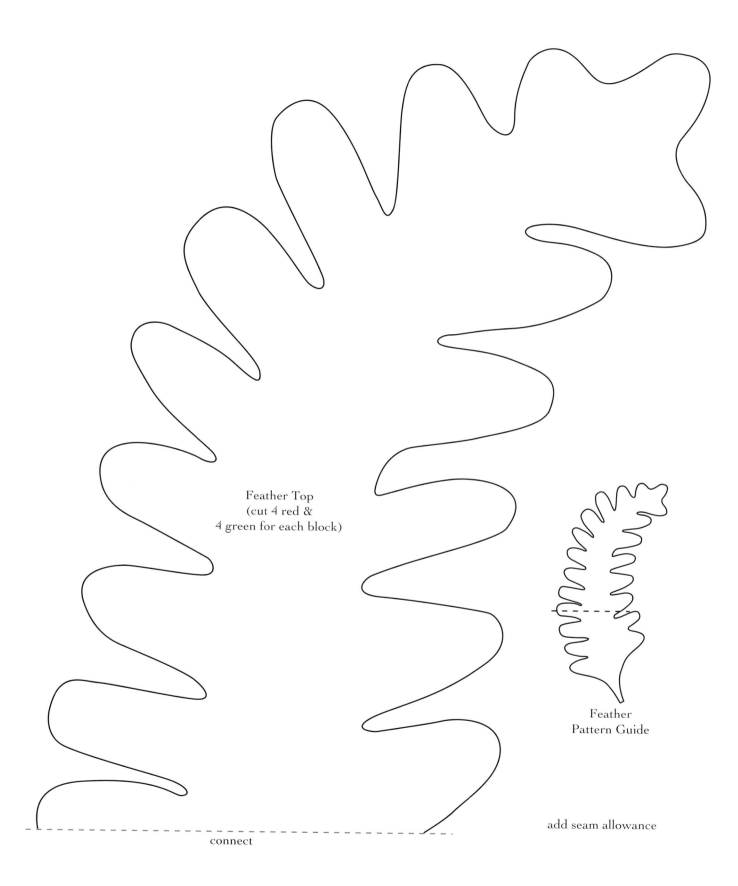

Feather Top
(cut 4 red &
4 green for each block)

Feather
Pattern Guide

add seam allowance

connect

Princess Feather

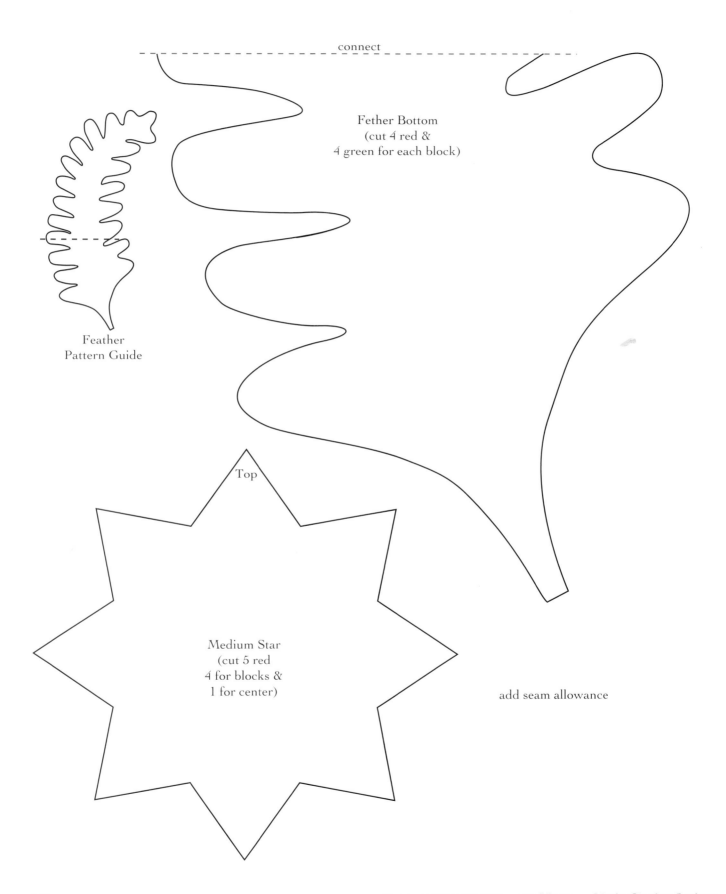

connect

Fether Bottom
(cut 4 red &
4 green for each block)

Feather
Pattern Guide

Top

Medium Star
(cut 5 red
4 for blocks &
1 for center)

add seam allowance

AMY'S WEDDING QUILT, 90" x 96", 1992. Made by the author and quilted by Katie Borntreger, Verona, Missouri. This large block was inspired by a multi-block quilt made in 1870 by 16-year-old Mary Parks Lawrence in Russellville, Kentucky. Photo by Richard Walker.

Fabric Requirements

8 yards of background color for blocks, borders, and binding

¼ yard of main vase color

⅞ yard of secondary vase color and 1 flower petal

1 yard for cherries and 1 flower petal color, center of heart

½ yard for flower centers, top, and bottom of vase

2½ yards green for leaves, stems, calyxes, border vine with bud branches

Make templates for pieced vase flowers, leaves, cherries, and vase parts. Remember to trace on the wrong side of the fabric for pieced flowers and vase. Trace templates on the right side of the fabric for individual leaves, cherries, vase top ring, vase handles, and vine bud branches. Make border leaf and bud branch templates. At times, these templates will be reversed to fit within the borders. Add seam allowance after tracing onto fabric.

Supplies

2 large sheets template plastic or freezer paper

Fabric scissors

Paper scissors

Template pencil

Piecing and appliqué needles

Threads to match fabrics

Fabric pencil

Embroidery thread for cherry stems

Batting and backing for 90" x 96" square

Cutting Instructions

(4) 36½" background blocks

(2) borders 12½" x 72½"

(2) borders 9½" x 96½"

(4) A, (4) B, (4) Br, (4) D, (4) E: main vase color

(8) C, (4) M, (4) Mr, (16) Q, (16) Qr: secondary vase color and one petal color

(4) F, (4) V, (4) O, (16) P: vase top and bottom color and flower centers

(64) G, (4) L, (4) Lr, (4) N, (4) Nr, (16) R, (16) Rr: flower petals and cherries

(4) H, (4) Hr, (4) I, (40) J, (4) K, (4) Kr, (16) S, (16) Sr, (4) T, (4) Tr, (4) U, (4) Ur: green stems, leaves, and calyxes

Border leaves and bud branches to fit undulating vine when concave and convex curves are determined

Two adult birds with wings from favorite scraps; reverse one so they face each other

Make as many baby bird grandchildren as you desire.

Make 2½" x 380" (ten 2½" x 44" strips) binding.

Block Assembly

Instructions are for one block. Repeat for other three blocks. See piecing diagram on page 83.

1. For the vase, piece the short bottoms of C pieces to each side of D.

2. Sew short bottom of A to top of first C.

3. Sew short top of E to long bottom of second C.

4. Sew F to bottom of E.

5. Pin the vase to the block about 2½" from the bottom center. Pin the handles under vase sides with top of handles even with top of A raw edge. Needle-turn the edges of the handles and appliqué.

6. Appliqué sides and bottom of the vase. Do not sew the top yet. *Option: Appliqué one of the adult birds under the side of the vase as if it were peering around the corner. Appliqué the other standing in front of another vase.*

7. To piece the vase flowers, sew the large center flower piece K to L, then L to M, M to N, then N to the right curved edge of O. Repeat for Kr to Lr, Lr to Mr, Mr to Nr, then Nr to the left side of O.

8. Join the bottom halves of the flower by butting the seam allowances of each color and having

raw edges somewhat even. Pin the marked lines at the end of the green calyx. Sew from bottom of O toward green calyx.

9. Piece the smaller flowers in the same way, sewing S to R, R to Q, and Q to the right side of P. Piece Sr to Rr, Rr to Qr, and Qr to the left side of P. Join the bottom halves of the small flowers in the same way as the previous flowers.

Attaching Vase Ring and Positioning Flowers (see page 83)

1. Position piece V around the top of the vase. About ¾" above the vase handles, tuck H and Hr under V. Appliqué the outside edge of the vase ring, folding under and catching the raw edges of H and Hr. Finish sewing H and Hr cherry branches. Position and pin center stem I, stems U and Ur, and stems T and Tr. Fold under raw edges and tuck seam ends under the front of the vase top ring. Stems should lay over the back of the vase ring. Needle-turn under edges of stems and appliqué. Either leave ¼" openings to tuck in leaf points, or plan to appliqué leaves with their ends just touching the stems.

2. Finger press under on the pieced flower edge pencil lines. Position and appliqué in place.

3. Appliqué two leaves to each stem.

4. Position and appliqué eight cherries around the cherry branches. Chain stitch the cherry stems from the branches to the cherries.

5. When all the blocks are done, stitch them together to form a 72½" square.

Center Appliqué (courtesy of Elly Sienkiewicz)

1. With a thick line, trace the heart and dove pattern onto freezer paper. Tape to a glass table or makeshift light table. Center the quilt top over the design and turn on light. Using a light touch and light lead pencil, carefully trace the design onto the quilt top.

2. Baste the right side of a 16" square of fabric used for cherries behind the heart and dove motif to the back of the quilt top.

3. Beginning with the doves, carefully cut away the top fabric only, a scant ¼" away from the drawn line. This is the turn-under allowance. Using thread to match the top fabric, reverse appliqué the raw edges to reveal the doves.

4. Starting at the bottom of the heart, carefully cut away top fabric inside the feathers to about ⅛" from the drawn line. Only cut a couple feathers at a time because pinning the resulting narrow bias feather edges is tedious. Needle-turn under the ⅛" seam allowance on the pencil line and reverse appliqué.

Borders

1. Lightly trace the undulating vine for the 12" wide border onto the right side of the 12½" x 72½" fabric border. Spread out on table or floor. Lay the 9½" x 96½" border, forming a right angle, on the left end of the drawn border.

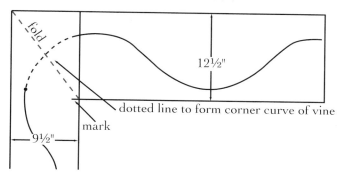

2. Lightly mark where the two borders meet at the inner corner. On the opposite side, 1¾" from the outside raw edge, mark a dot. This is where you start tracing the undulating vine for the 9½" x 96½" border.

3. Before tracing the vine for the longer side border, make a diagonal fold from the mark where the two

borders meet on the inside corner to the outside corner. Finger press. This will help you visualize the highest point of the corner curve of the vine. Lightly draw a dotted line connecting the two vines in the corner curve. Repeat for the remaining borders.

4. Make continuous bias strips to finish at 2¼" in width. A total of about 450" in length is needed to accommodate the large curves in the vine.

5. Fold and iron the bias in half, wrong sides together. Position the raw edges a scant ¼" over the drawn line on the border. Pin several inches and sew the bias strip about ⅛" below the drawn line. Use small stitches because this will be finished when it is folded up and over the raw bias edges and appliquéd.

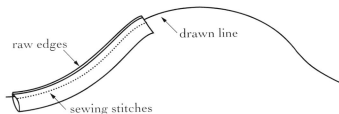

raw edges

drawn line

sewing stitches

6. Position the border leaves and bud branches within the convex and concave curves now if you want to catch their stems as you sew the vine. Otherwise, plan to abut the stems next to the vine after it is sewn. Remember to reverse leaf and bud branch templates to accommodate curves.

7. Appliqué and reverse appliqué buds as needed. Appliqué as many baby bird grandchildren as you hope to have in the corners and on the vines.

8. Sew the borders to quilt, top and bottom first, then the sides.

Finishing

1. Mark the quilting lines. Layer the backing, batting, and quilt top.

2. Baste and quilt as desired.

3. Apply the binding following general directions, page 23.

Quilt Assembly

Block Assembly

Amy's Wedding Quilt

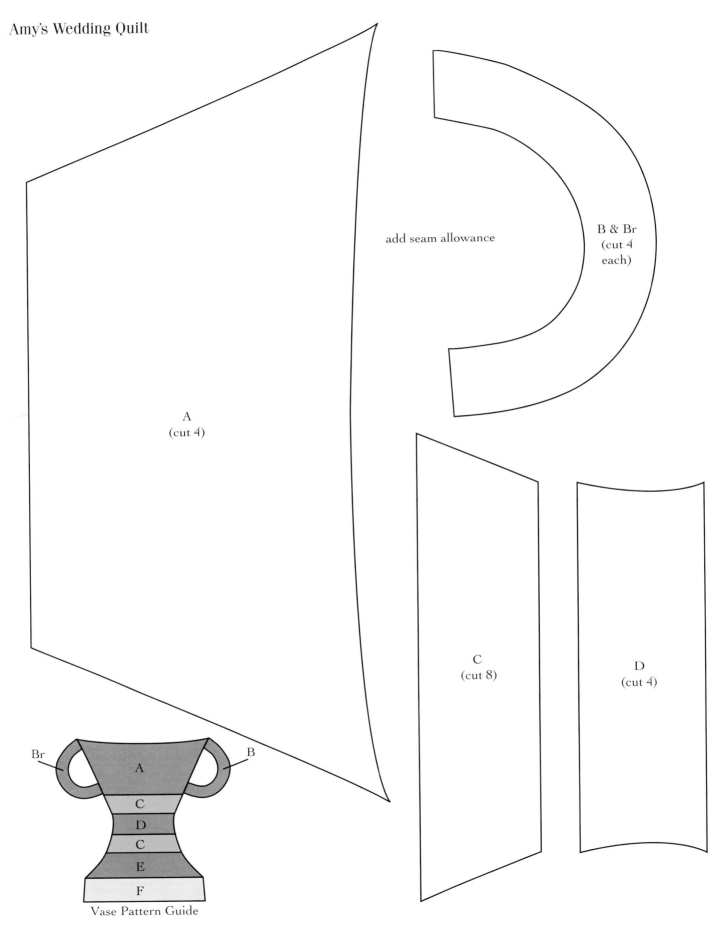

add seam allowance

B & Br
(cut 4 each)

A
(cut 4)

C
(cut 8)

D
(cut 4)

Br   B

A

C

D

C

E

F

Vase Pattern Guide

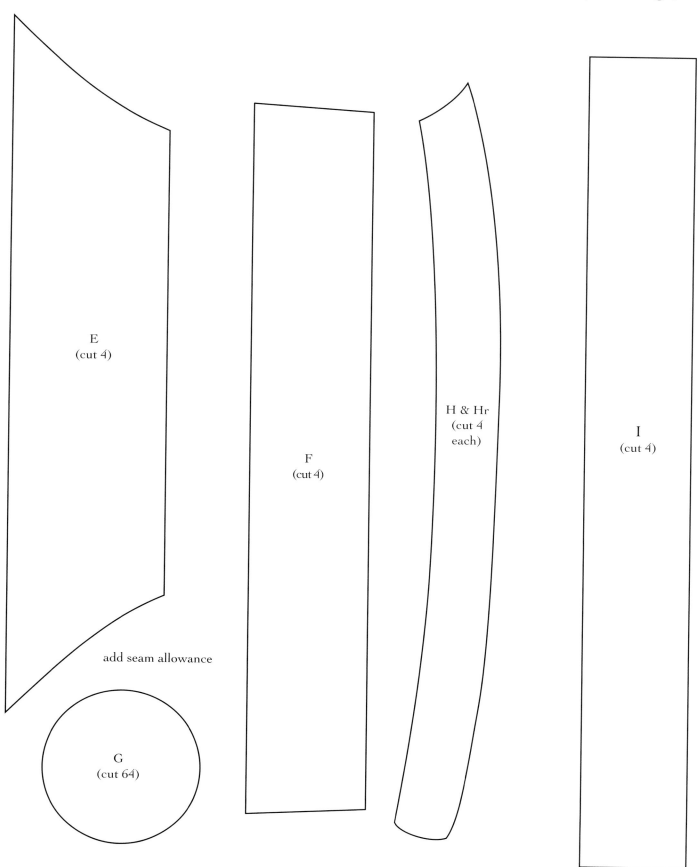

E
(cut 4)

add seam allowance

G
(cut 64)

F
(cut 4)

H & Hr
(cut 4
each)

I
(cut 4)

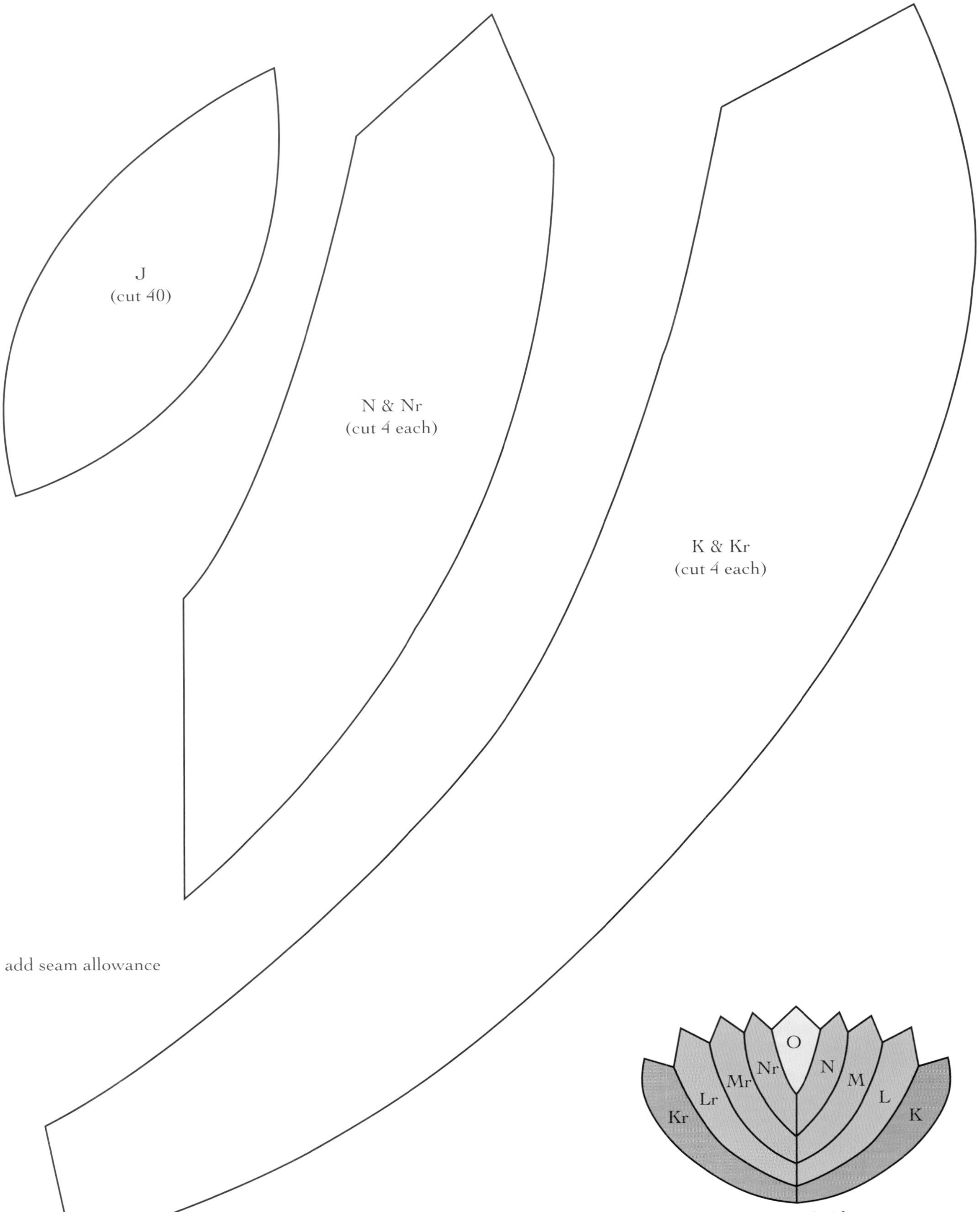
J
(cut 40)
N & Nr
(cut 4 each)
K & Kr
(cut 4 each)
add seam allowance
O
Nr
N
Mr
M
Lr
L
Kr
K

Pattern Guide

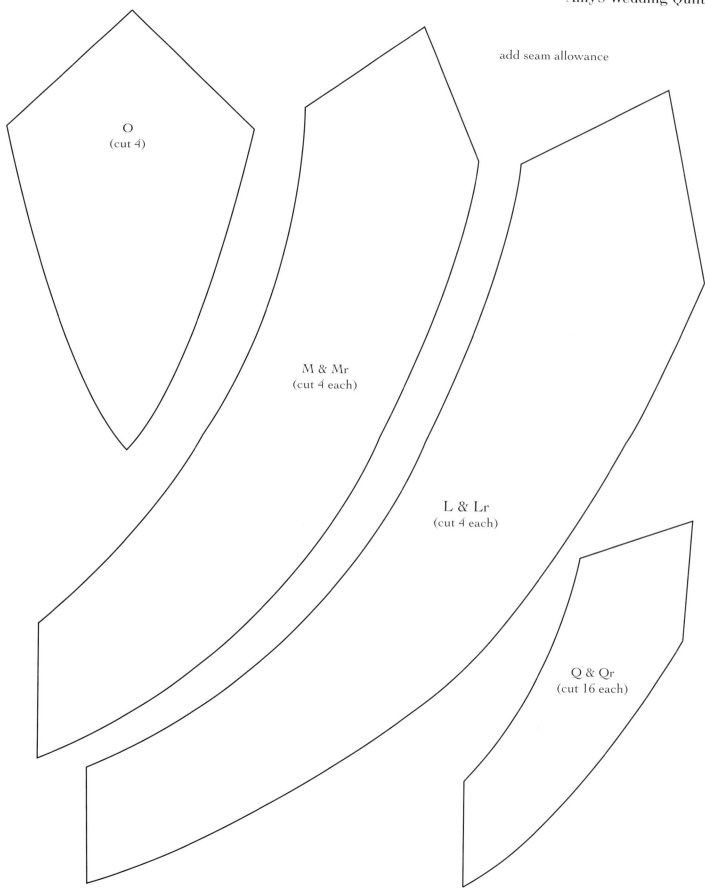

add seam allowance

O
(cut 4)

M & Mr
(cut 4 each)

L & Lr
(cut 4 each)

Q & Qr
(cut 16 each)

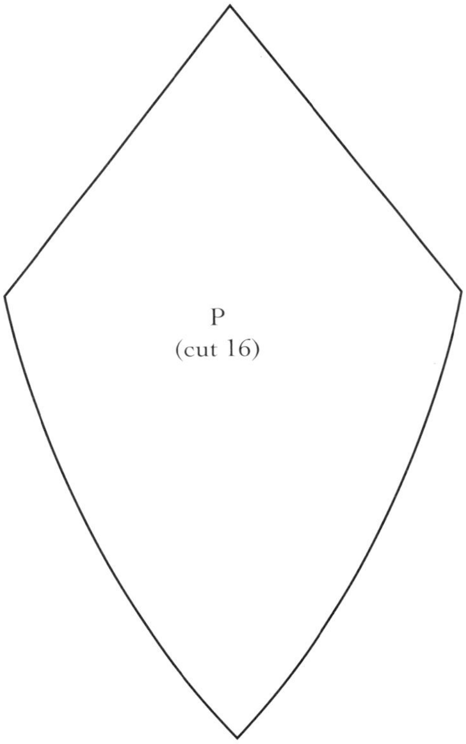

Amy's Wedding Quilt

P
(cut 16)

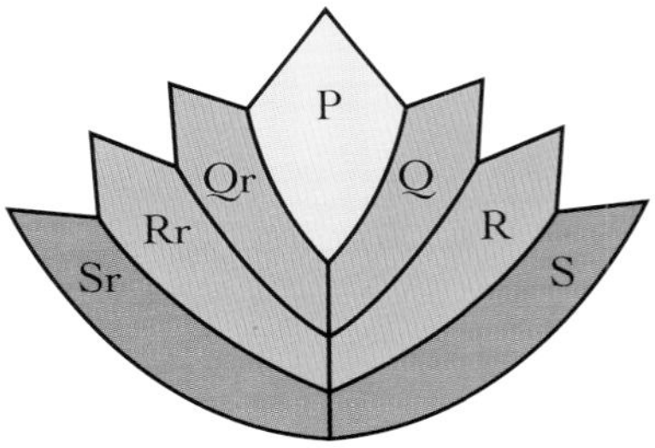

Pattern Guide

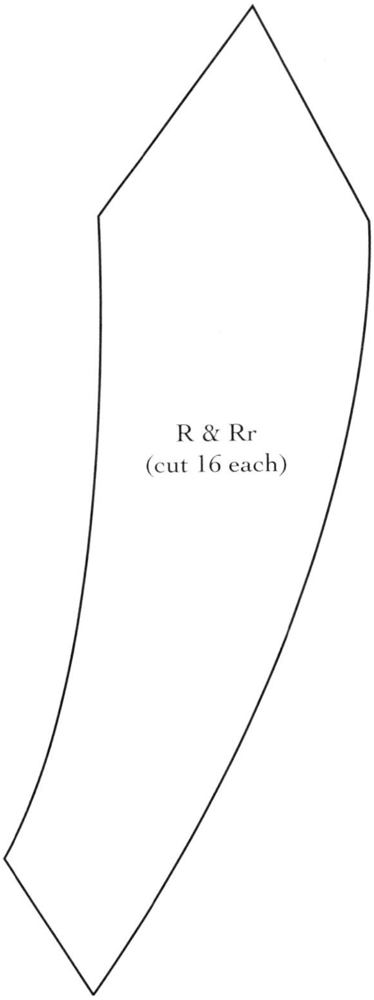

R & Rr
(cut 16 each)

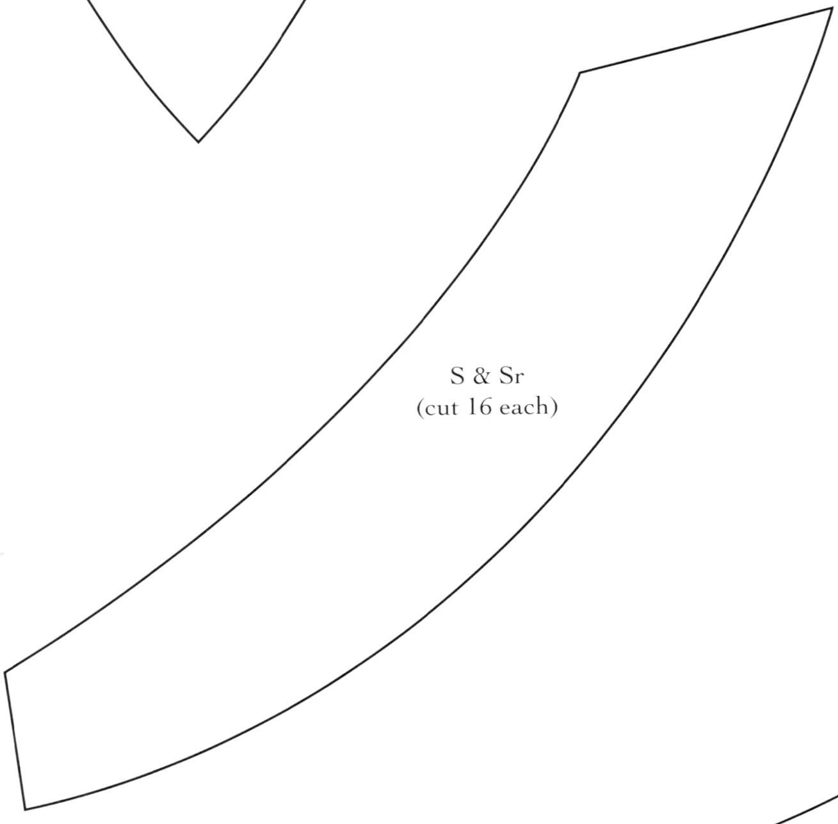

S & Sr
(cut 16 each)

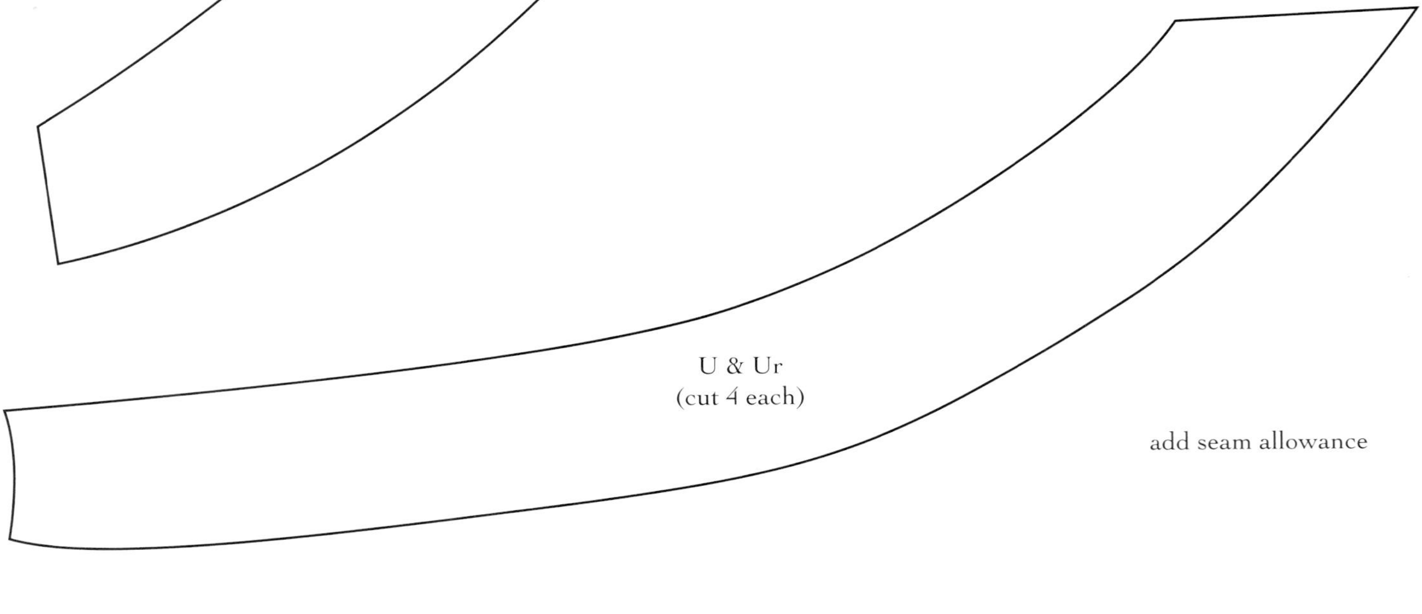

U & Ur
(cut 4 each)

add seam allowance

BEST OF FOUR BLOCKS…AND MORE   Linda Giesler Carlson

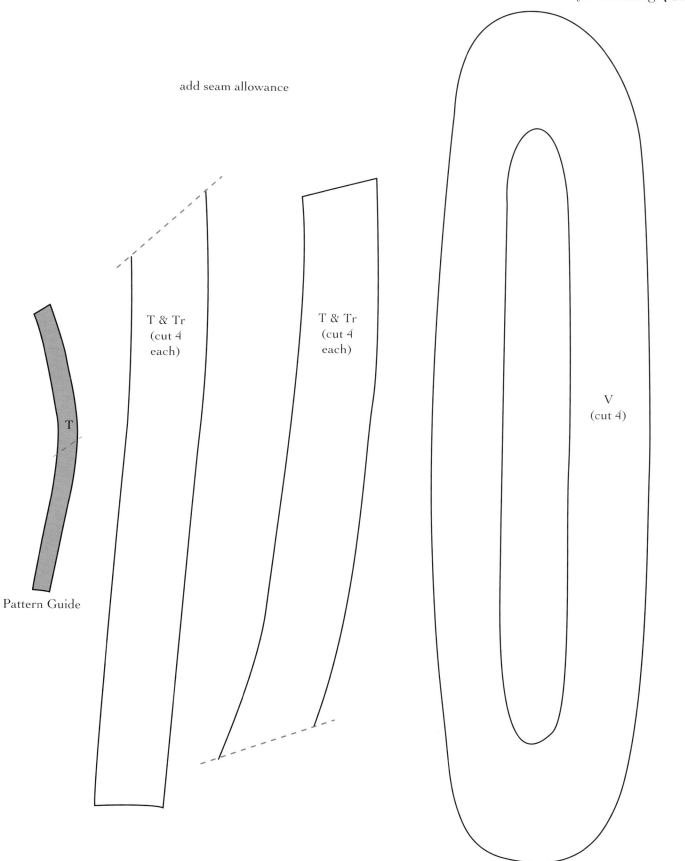

Amy's Wedding Quilt

add seam allowance

T & Tr
(cut 4
each)

T & Tr
(cut 4
each)

V
(cut 4)

T

Pattern Guide

Pattern Guide

This original design by Elly Sienkiewicz is one of 24 patterns in her *Baltimore Beauties and Beyond, Studies in Classic Baltimore Album Quilts, Volume 1* (C&T Publishing, 1989). It is reprinted here with her permission.

add seam allowance

reverse pattern here

Feather-Wreathed Heart
with Doves

connect pattern on page 91

add seam allowance

Feather-Wreathed Heart
with Doves

connect pattern on page 90

reverse pattern here

Amy's Wedding Quilt

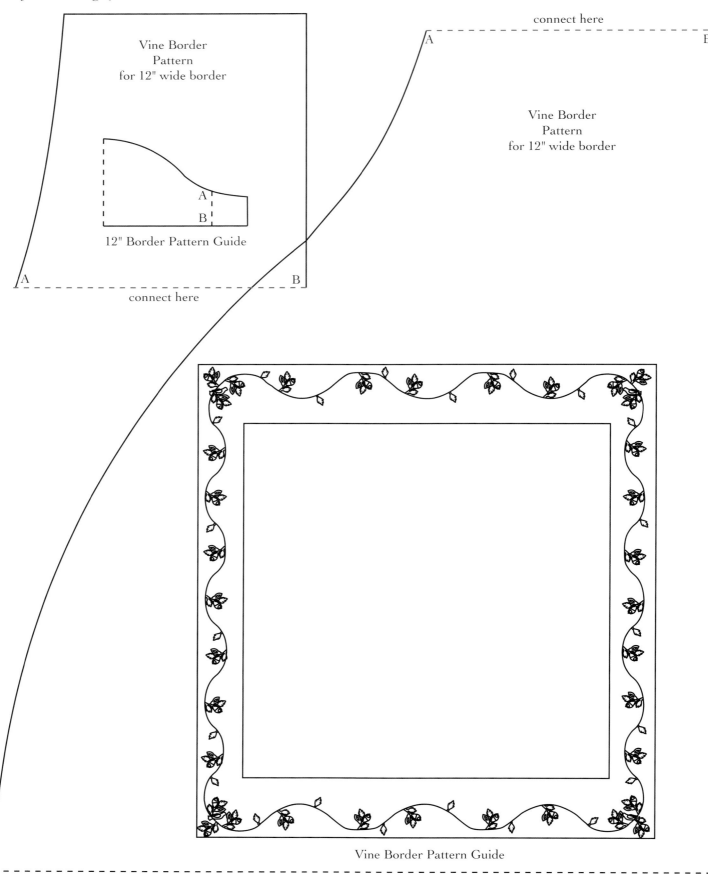

Vine Border
Pattern
for 12" wide border

A

B

12" Border Pattern Guide

A

connect here

B

connect here

Vine Border
Pattern
for 12" wide border

A

B

Vine Border Pattern Guide

add seam allowance

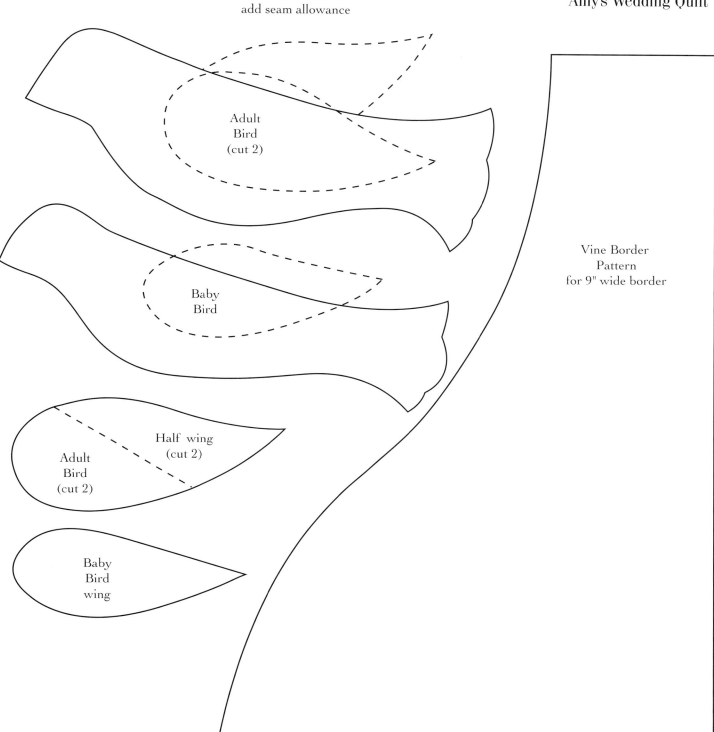

Adult
Bird
(cut 2)

Baby
Bird

Vine Border
Pattern
for 9" wide border

Adult
Bird
(cut 2)

Half wing
(cut 2)

Baby
Bird
wing

1a
(cut 18 and
cut 18 reverse)

cut out

2b

1a

Pattern Guide

3c
cut
out

Bud
2b
(cut 36)

add seam allowance

3c
bud color
(cut 36)
lay under bud

4d
(cut 11 and
cut 11 reverse)

Amish Rose

of Sharon Wreath – An Ode to Sara Miller

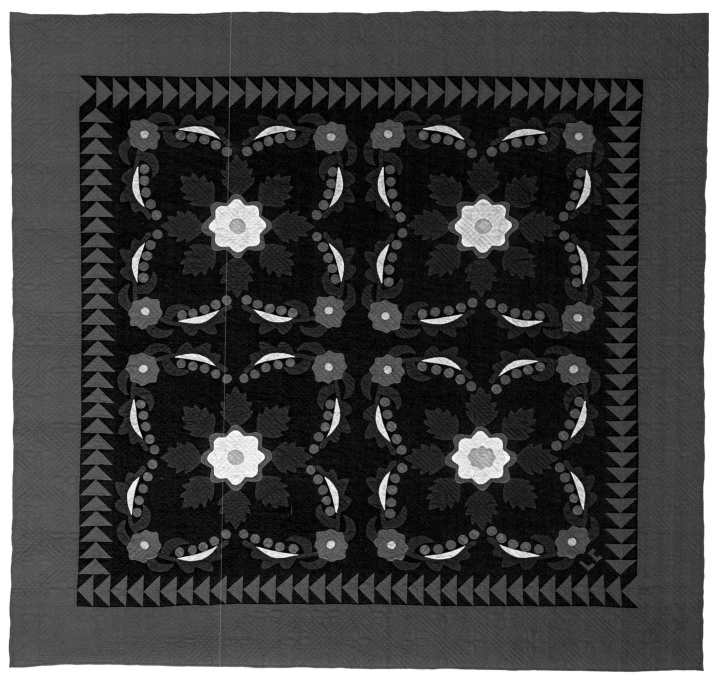

AMISH ROSE OF SHARON WREATH, 84" x 84", 1997. Made by the author. This quilt is a tribute to Sara Miller, Kalona, Iowa.

Fabric Requirements

Colors represent a traditional Amish color palette.

4½ yards dark green

2½ yards red

2½ yards bright red

2¼ yards medium green

¾ yard red stripe

¾ yard red for binding

¼ yard pink

¼ yard gold

½ yard light green

Supplies

Basic sewing kit, page 21

Backing for 84" block

Batting for 84" block

Cutting Instructions

Instructions on the pattern pieces are for one block, unless otherwise noted.

(4) 30½" dark green blocks

(2) 8½" x 68½" red borders

(2) 8½" x 84½" red borders

Straight-grain strips to equal 2¼" x 345"
(eight 2¼" x 44" strips) red for binding

(4) red stripe A

(4) pink B

(3) gold C

(1) gold D

(32) medium green E

(16) red F

(16) gold G

(16) medium green H and (16) medium green Hr

(16) light green I and (16) light green Ir

(16) medium green J and (16) medium green Jr

(32) medium green K and (32) medium green Kr

(80) red stripe L; (40) red L; and (40) bright red L

(32) 5¼" x 5¼" bright red square Unit 1's for Flying Geese border

(128) 2⅞" x 2⅞" dark green Unit 2's for Flying Geese

Trace all templates on the right side of the fabric. Add an ⅛" seam allowance on all pieces.

Block Assembly

1. Fold a 30½" x 30½" block into quarters to find the center. Finger press.

2. Center and pin A over the block center, and align it with the four folds.

3. Insert eight E pieces under the convex petals. Appliqué these first, then the (A) rose.

4. Carefully cut out the back of the block ¼" inside the appliqué stitches to facilitate quilting later.

5. Place and pin the B over A. Appliqué in place. Cut out the back again, leaving a ¼" seam allowance.

6. Place C on the B rose. Appliqué in place, but do not cut out the back. Substitute D for C on the last block.

7. In the quilt photo, page 95, notice how the corner roses (F) are placed in the blocks. Measure diagonally from the corner edge 3¼" and pin F there.

8. Insert G rose center for reverse appliqué and pin. Place the J and Jr stems in the correct positions. Pin the K and Kr rose leaves in place. Loosely baste with long running stitches down the piece center. Remove all pins.

9. Pin the H and Hr leaves and the I and Ir pods on each side of the corner rose. Match the pod tip to the mark on the leaf. Template instructions are on page 21. The leaf will be appliquéd over the bottom curve of the pod. Loosely baste the leaves and the pods. Appliqué them to the block.

10. Pin five L cherries above each H-I unit. Appliqué in place.

11. Repeat steps for each block. Join the four blocks.

Flying Geese Inner Border

1. Follow assembly instructions on page 22 and make 128 Flying Geese units.

2. Once the Flying Geese squares have been completed, sew 30 Flying Geese units together so that they are all pointing the same direction. Attach this band to the top of the quilt by matching the center of the Flying Geese band to the quilt center seam. Pin outward. Sew using a ¼" seam allowance on the sewing machine. Repeat for the bottom, with the geese flying in the opposite direction.

3. Sew 34 Flying Geese units together for the side border. Match and pin from the center outward. Be sure the direction of the geese units continues the direction of the top and bottom borders and does not reverse it. Sew with a ¼" seam allowance.

4. Repeat for the other side border. Remember to check the geese direction.

Outer Borders

1. Fold an 8½" x 68½" red border to find the center. Finger press. Match fold to the quilt side center seam. Pin outward. Sew.

2. Repeat for the opposite side border.

3. Fold to find the center of the 8½" x 84½" top and bottom borders. Pin from the center seam outward. Sew.

Finishing

1. Mark the quilting lines. Layer the batting, backing, and top. Baste.

2. Quilt closely and consistently, which is a hallmark of Amish quilts.

3. Apply binding following the general directions, page 23.

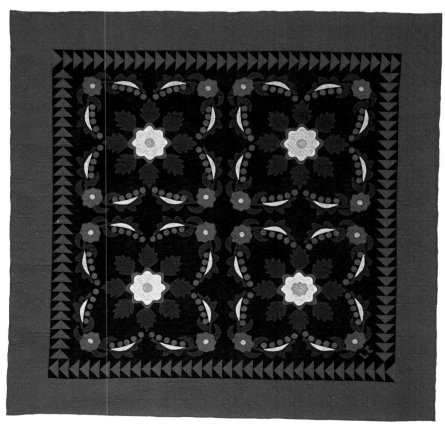

Amish Rose of Sharon

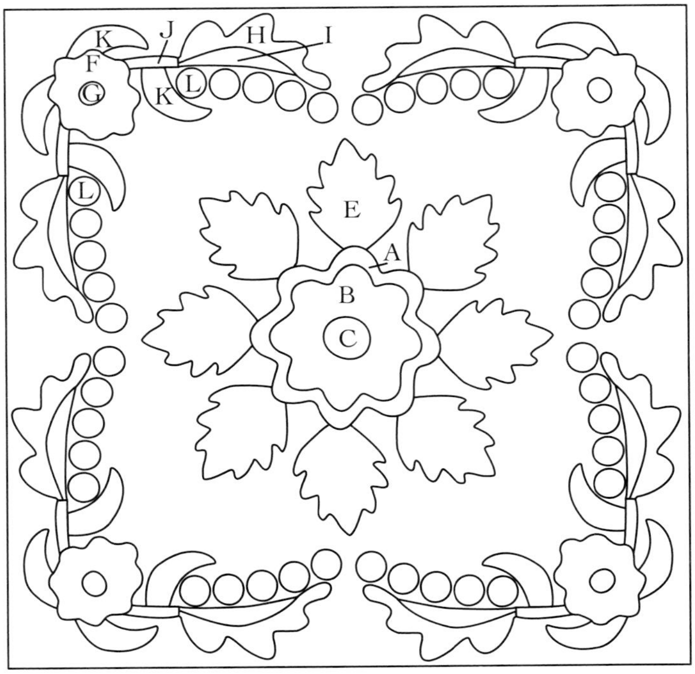
K
J
H
I
F
G
K
L
L
E
A
B
C

Block Assembly

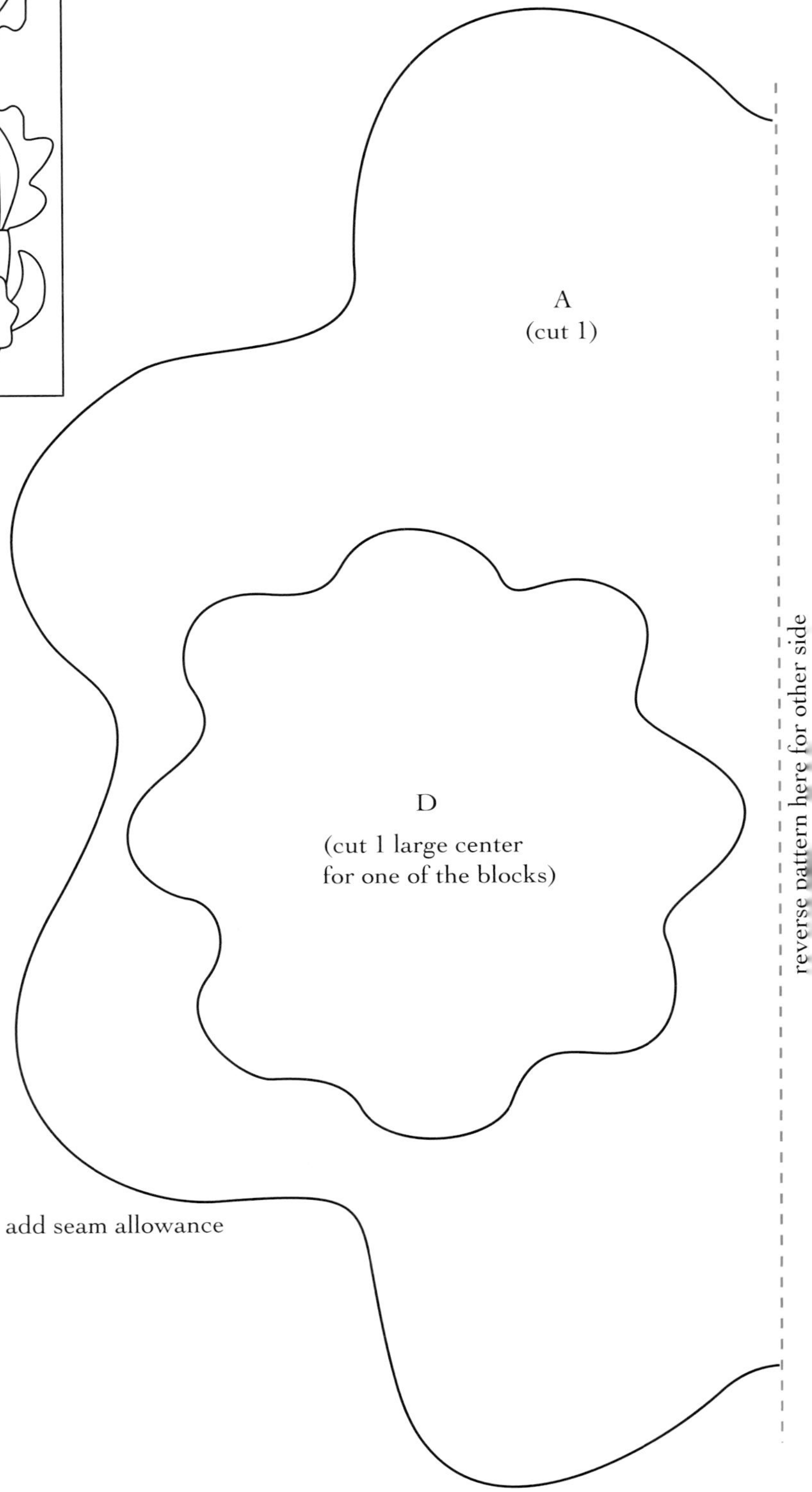
A
(cut 1)
D
(cut 1 large center
for one of the blocks)
add seam allowance
reverse pattern here for other side

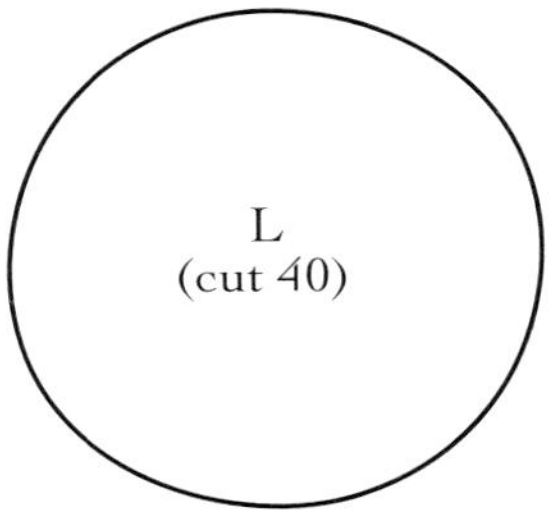
L
(cut 40)

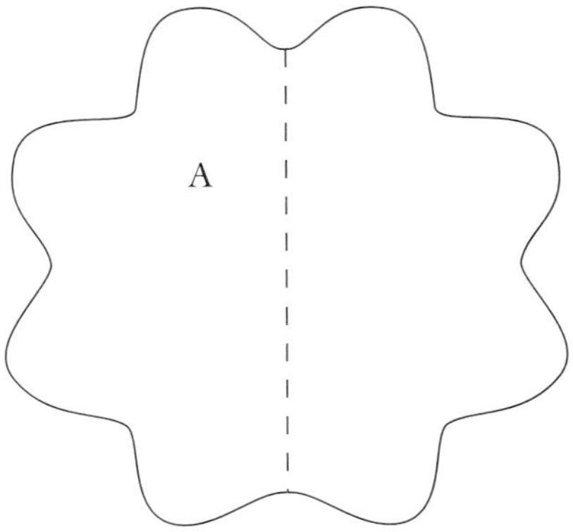
A

Pattern Guide

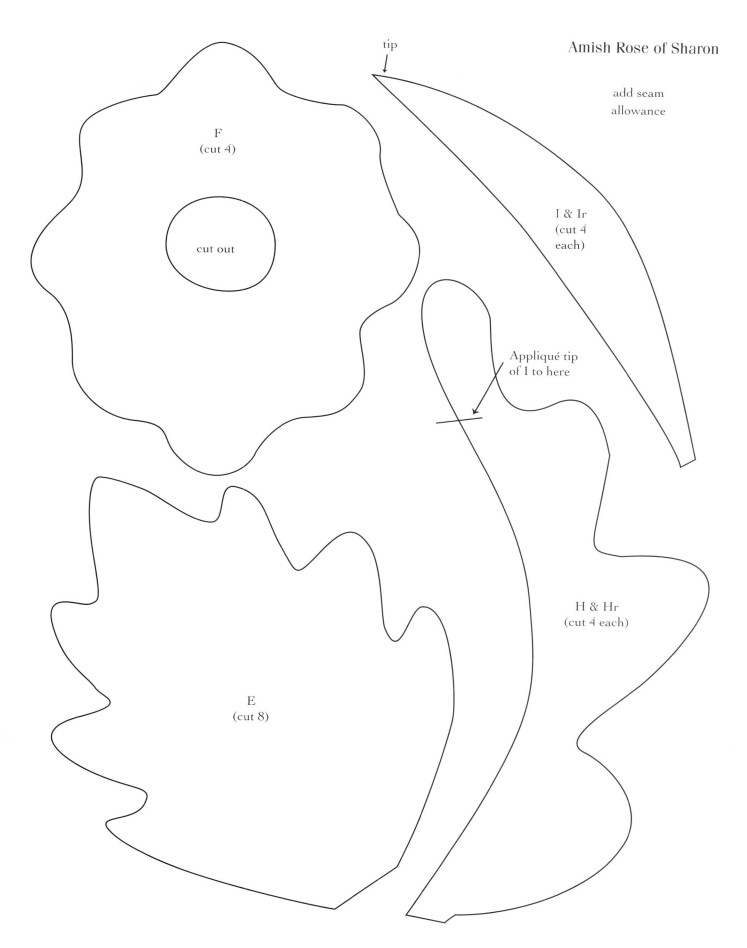

tip

Amish Rose of Sharon

add seam allowance

F
(cut 4)

cut out

I & Ir
(cut 4
each)

Appliqué tip
of I to here

H & Hr
(cut 4 each)

E
(cut 8)

Amish Rose of Sharon

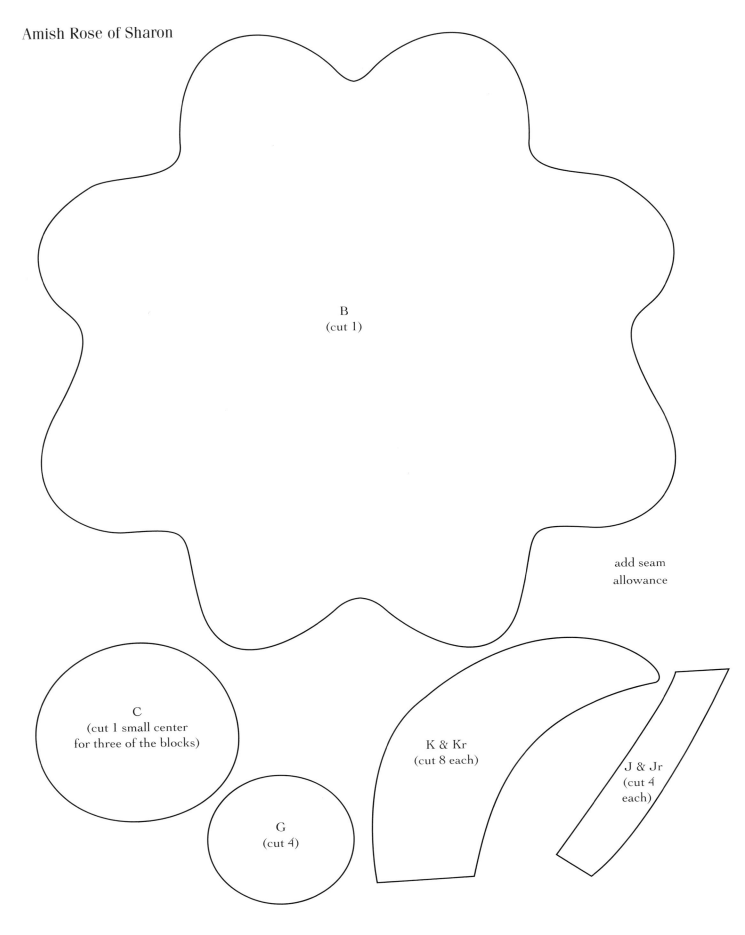

B
(cut 1)

add seam
allowance

C
(cut 1 small center
for three of the blocks)

K & Kr
(cut 8 each)

J & Jr
(cut 4
each)

G
(cut 4)

BEST OF FOUR BLOCKS…AND MORE   *Linda Giesler Carlson*

Philadelphia
Centennial Four-Block Eagle

1776–1876 PHILADELPHIA CENTENNIAL EAGLE, 79" x 79", made in Pennsylvania, 1870–1876. The appliqué patterns in this project were taken directly from the quilt and are not symmetrical, adding to the quilt's stately charm. The sawtooth border instructions vary from the quilt photograph to fit the block sizes given.

Fabric Requirements

5½ yards orange
1½ yards green
1½ yards red
½ yard yellow

Supplies

Basic sewing kit, page 21
Batting for 79" square
Backing for 79" square

Cutting Instructions

Instructions on the pattern pieces are for one block.
unless otherwise noted.

(4) orange 30½" blocks
(2) orange 8½" x 63½" borders
(2) orange 8½" x 79½" borders
Make 2¼" x 325" (eight 2¼" x 44" strips)
    orange straight-grain binding
(4) green A and (4) green Ar
(4) red B
(4) yellow C
(4) green D
(4) red E
(4) red F and (4) red Fr
(4) red G
(1) red H
(1) green I
(1) 26" orange square for sawtooth squares
(1) 26" red square for sawtooth squares

Cut out all appliqué pieces with an ⅛" seam
allowance.

Block Assembly

1. The eagles do not have to be symmetrically posi-
tioned. Fold a 30½" block on the diagonal both
ways and finger press. Position A and Ar in
opposite corners. Position B so that it generally
points to the center corner and so G will point
toward the lower outer corner. Adjust according-
ly so C will cover the seam allowance on the
lower head, wings, and tail.

2. Needle-turn appliqué the wing edges. Appliqué
the head, leaving the beak and neck open. Iron

the long side seam allowances on D. Pin it into
the eagle's beak and appliqué E to the top of D.

3. Position and pin F, Fr, and G in place. Turn under
the seam allowances where these pieces go under
C. Appliqué the shield, then the feet and tail.

4. Appliqué the remaining three blocks likewise.
Join two blocks so that the eagles face the center. Repeat for the other two blocks. Join the
four blocks by matching the center seams and
pinning outward. Sew.

5. Pin H over the center. Pin I over H. Appliqué the
small star, then the large star.

Sawtooth Borders

Using the requirements listed below, follow the
instructions on pages 21 and 22 to make 124 sawtooth squares.

1. Draw a grid of 2⅞" squares, eight rows by eight
columns.

2. With a ¼" seam allowance, sew two borders of
30 sawtooth squares each for the top and bottom inner borders. Sew two
borders of 32 sawtooth
squares each for the side
inner borders. Because the
red tooth will be next to the
outer borders on all sides,
make sure that you stitch the
units together as shown.

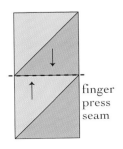

finger
press
seam

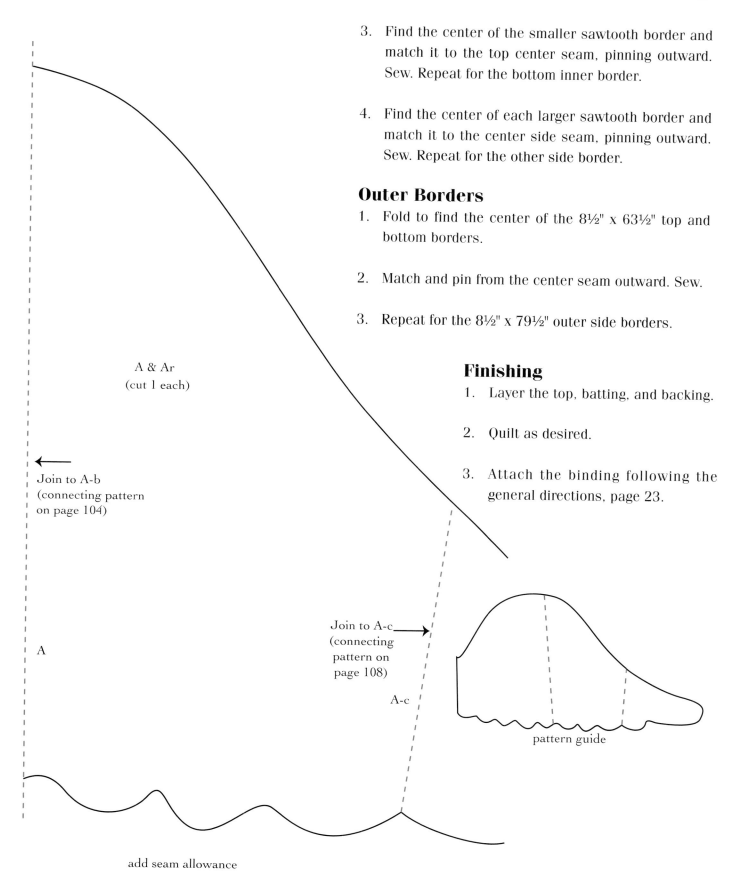

3. Find the center of the smaller sawtooth border and match it to the top center seam, pinning outward. Sew. Repeat for the bottom inner border.

4. Find the center of each larger sawtooth border and match it to the center side seam, pinning outward. Sew. Repeat for the other side border.

Outer Borders

1. Fold to find the center of the 8½" x 63½" top and bottom borders.

2. Match and pin from the center seam outward. Sew.

3. Repeat for the 8½" x 79½" outer side borders.

Finishing

1. Layer the top, batting, and backing.

2. Quilt as desired.

3. Attach the binding following the general directions, page 23.

A & Ar
(cut 1 each)

← Join to A-b
(connecting pattern
on page 104)

A

Join to A-c
(connecting
pattern on
page 108)

A-c

pattern guide

add seam allowance

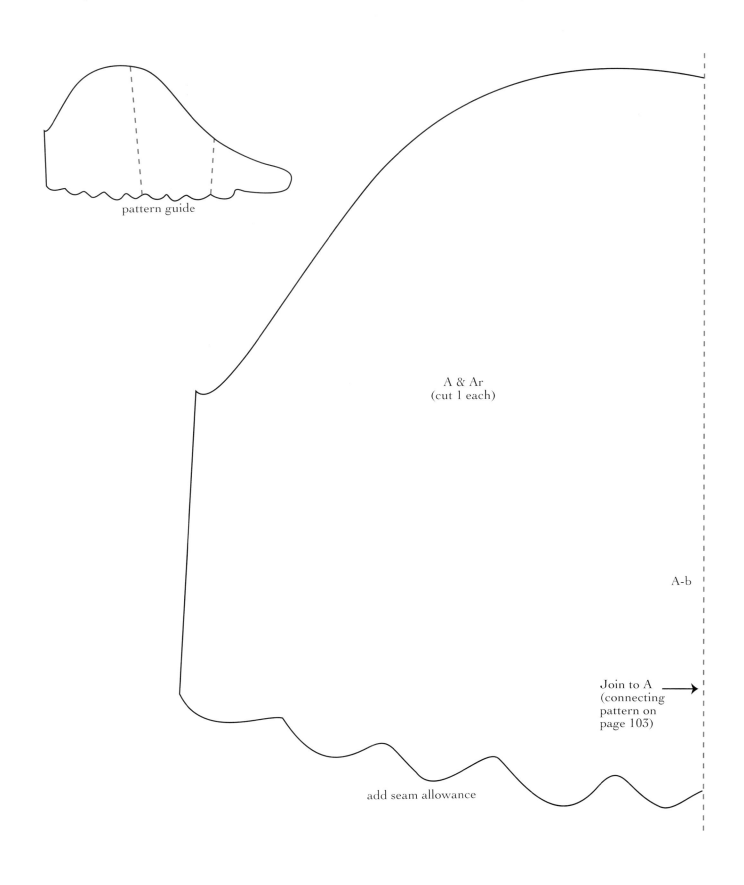

pattern guide

A & Ar
(cut 1 each)

A-b

Join to A →
(connecting
pattern on
page 103)

add seam allowance

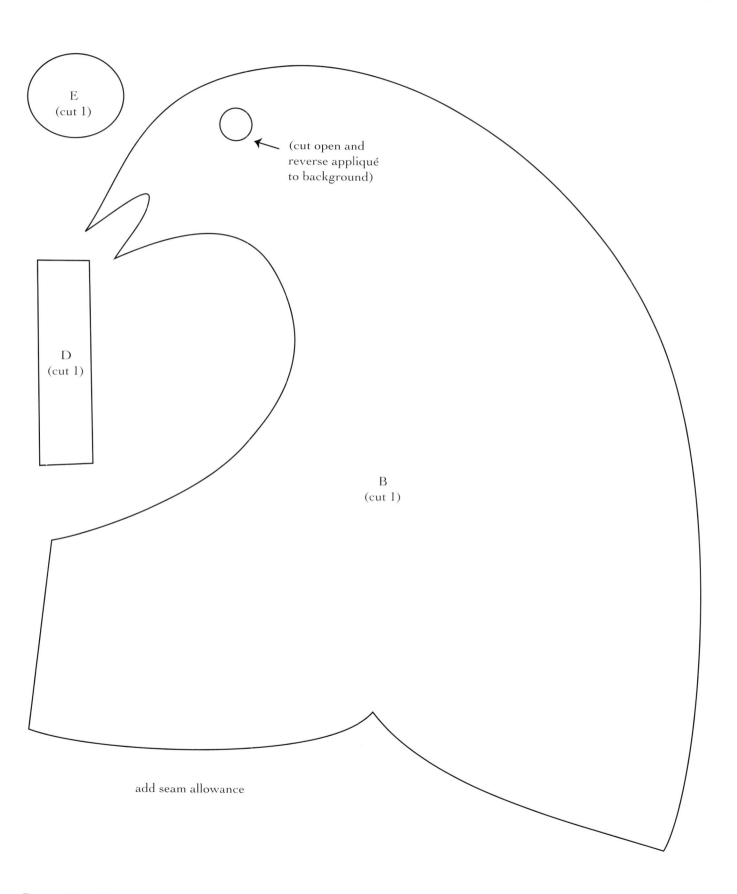

E
(cut 1)

(cut open and
reverse appliqué
to background)

D
(cut 1)

B
(cut 1)

add seam allowance

Philadelphia Centennial Four-Block Eagle

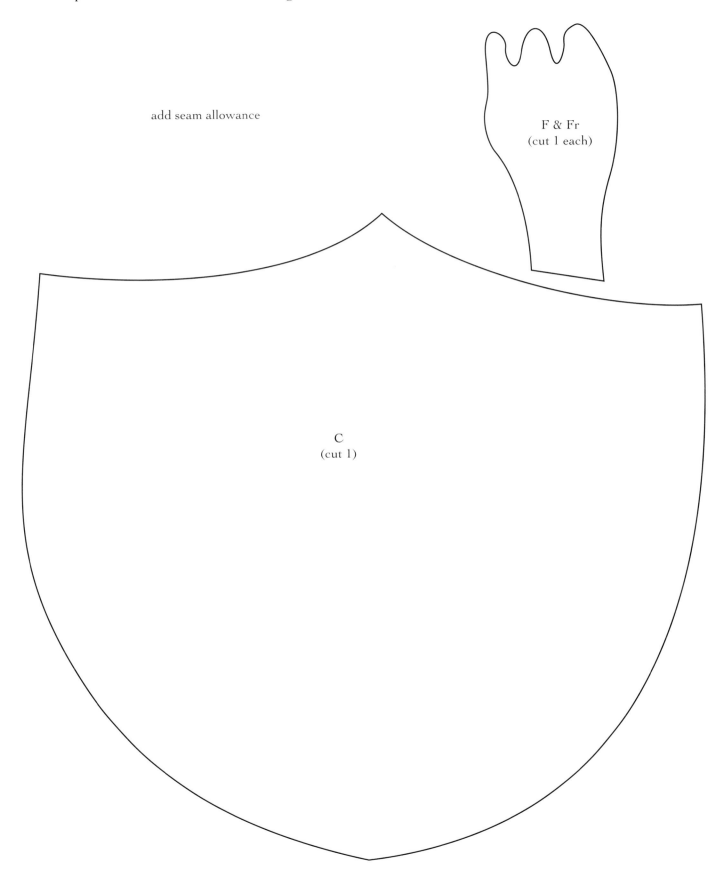

add seam allowance

F & Fr
(cut 1 each)

C
(cut 1)

BEST OF FOUR BLOCKS...AND MORE   *Linda Giesler Carlson*

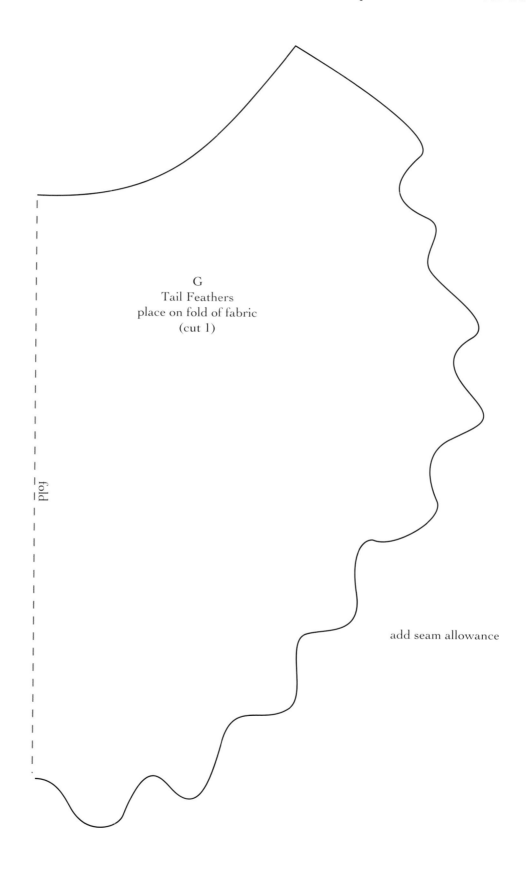

G
Tail Feathers
place on fold of fabric
(cut 1)

fold

add seam allowance

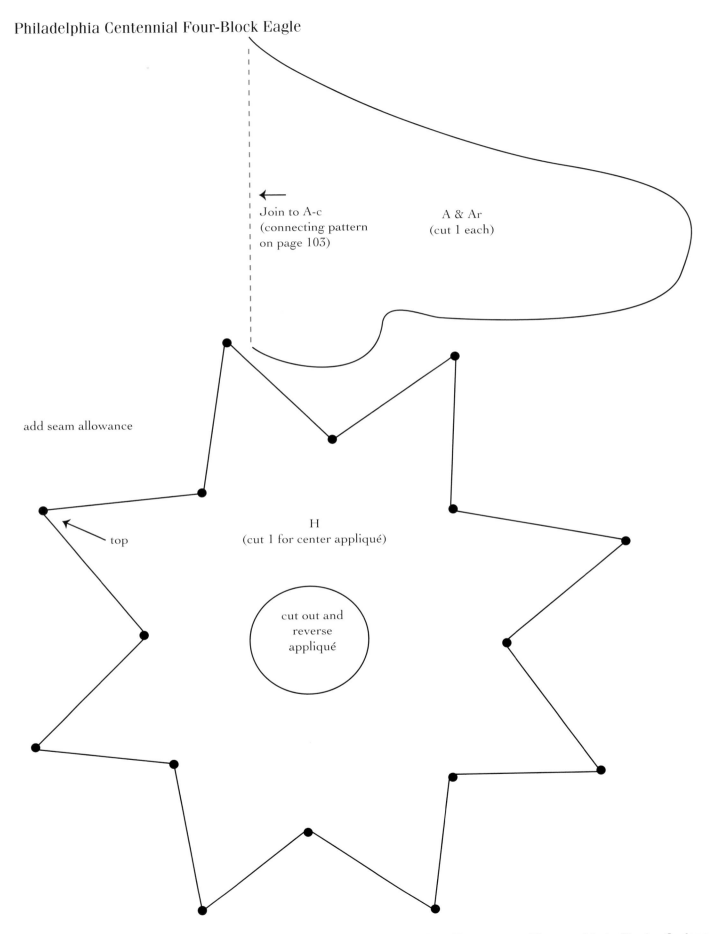

Join to A-c
(connecting pattern
on page 103)

A & Ar
(cut 1 each)

add seam allowance

top

H
(cut 1 for center appliqué)

cut out and
reverse
appliqué

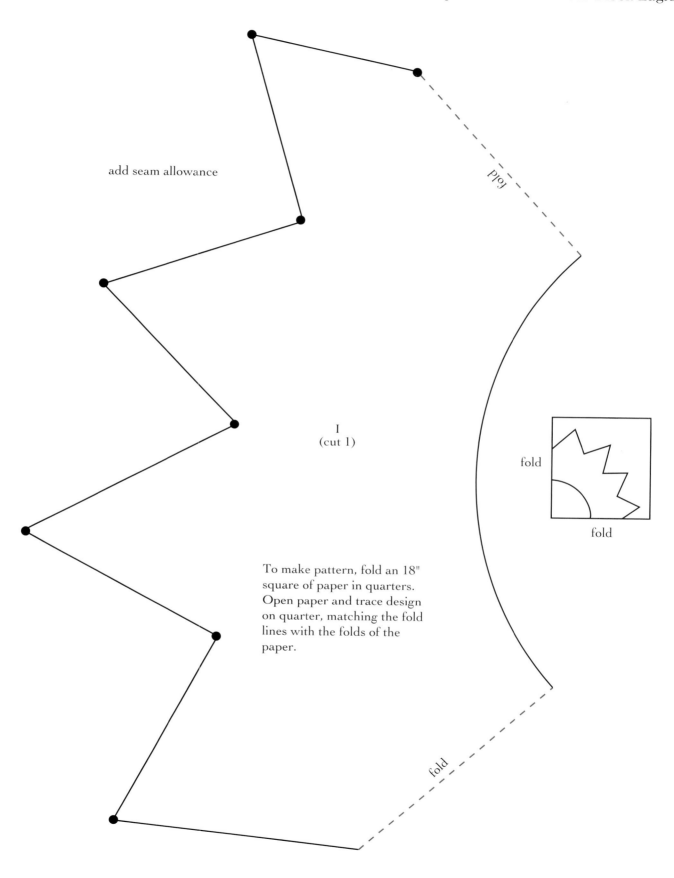

add seam allowance

fold

I
(cut 1)

fold

fold

To make pattern, fold an 18"
square of paper in quarters.
Open paper and trace design
on quarter, matching the fold
lines with the folds of the
paper.

fold

GORDIAN KNOT, 76" x 76", made in Cumberland County, Pennsylvania, ca. 1920. This pattern is also known as Mystic Maze. The author simplified this quilt design to a traditiional machine-pieced Log Cabin with the rotary strip technique. Her best friend, Roslyn Dial, drafted the pattern. There is no need to cut hundreds of rectangles.

Fabric Requirements

4½ yards white
2½ yards blue

Supplies

Basic sewing kit, page 21
Batting and backing for 76" square

Cutting Instructions

(2) white 8½" x 60½" borders
(2) white 8½" x 76½" borders
(16) white 2½" squares
(4) white 4½" squares
(16) white 4½" x 7½" rectangles
(2) white 4½" x 28½" sashing
(1) white 4½" x 60½" sashing
(4) blue 2" x 76½" strips for the appliqué dogtooth binding

Cut out all borders, squares, rectangles, and sashing. Cut (24) blue 1½" wide strips and (10) white 1½" wide strips from the remaining fabric.

Unit Assembly

Unit #1

The circled numbers on the diagram indicate the order of attachment.

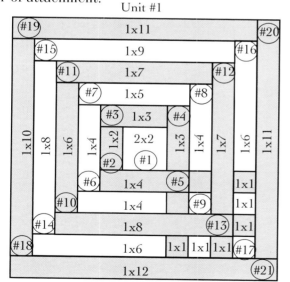

Unit #1

1. Start with the #1 white 2½" square. Sew a blue strip to it. Trim the threads. With the right sides together, trim the #2 blue strip even with the #1 white square.

2. Open to the right side. Finger press. Sew a blue strip in the #3 position. Trim even with the #2 edge.

3. Finger press open. Sew a blue strip in the #4 position. Trim even.

4. Finger press open. Sew a blue strip in the #5 position. Trim even.

5. Using the same method as in steps 1–4, attach a white strip in the #6 and #7 positions.

6. From the strips, cut a 4½" white strip and a 1½" blue square. Sew them together and attach the unit in the #8 position.

7. Sew a 1½" white square to a 1½" blue square, then a 4½" white strip. Sew the unit in the #9 position.

8. Sew a blue strip into the #10, #11, #12, and #13 positions.

9. Sew a white strip in the #14 and #15 positions.

10. For position #16, assemble a 6½" white strip, 1½" blue square, 1½" white square, and then another 1½" blue square. Sew into place.

11. For position #17, assemble the squares, white, blue, white, blue, then a 6½" white strip. Sew into place.

12. Sew blue strips into the #18, #19, #20, and #21 positions.

13. Repeat steps to make four #1 units.

Unit #2: 4" x 7" White Rectangle

Unit #3: Five-Strip Unit

1. Alternate blue and white 1½" x 4½" strips to form a five-strip unit as shown.

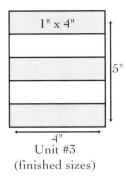

1" x 4"

5"

4"
Unit #3
(finished sizes)

2. Repeat Step 1 to make three more #3 units.

Block Assembly

1. Sew units 2 and 3 together. Make four 2-3 units.

2. Sew a complete 2-3 unit to the side of Unit 1.

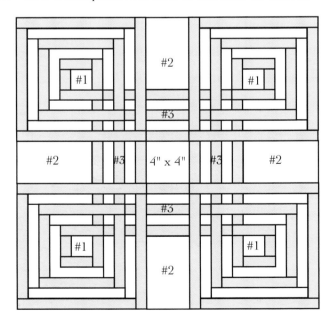

3. Sew another Unit 1 to the opposite side of the 2-3 unit.

4. Sew a 2-3 unit to the 4½" square, then to another 2-3 unit, forming a sash.

5. Matching the vertical seams, pin the sashing to the upper half of the block and sew.

6. Repeat steps 2 and 3 to form the bottom half of the block.

7. Join the bottom half to the sashing, matching the vertical seams.

Joining the Blocks

1. Sew two blocks to each vertical side of the 4½" x 28½" sashing. Join the other two blocks in the same manner.

2. Find the center of the 4½" x 60½" sashing. Finger press. Pin from the center, working outward to the top two blocks. Sew. Pin and sew to the bottom two blocks.

3. Find the center of the 8½" x 60½" upper border. Match to the top center of the quilt top; pin working outward. Sew. Match the bottom border. Pin from the center outward; sew.

4. Find the center of each 8½" x 76½" side border. Match and pin from the center outward; sew.

Finishing

1. Mark the quilting design.

2. Layer the backing, batting, and top.

3. Baste and quilt as desired.

Appliqué Dogtooth Binding

1. Mark dots on the strips as shown on page 113. Start by making a dot ½" in from both ends of the strip and 1¼" from the top. Repeat dots every 1½". Mark offset dots on the raw edge with the first dot 1¼" from the end of the strip. Repeat dots every 1½".

2. Cut down 1¼" at the lower line dots.

3. With right sides together, pin the binding to the back edge of the quilt top. Sew with a ½" seam allowance.

4. Fold the binding up and over the quilt top. Needle-turn under the vertical and horizontal raw edges of the ½" beginning indentation about ⅛" and appliqué.

5. Fold under the right side of the first dogtooth ⅛". Appliqué to the background within ¹⁄₁₆" of the marked dot. Take two stitches to anchor the point, then push the remaining raw edge toward the left side of the dogtooth and under the anchored point. Continue to appliqué the left side of the dogtooth. Take two stitches at the inner dot 1¼" down and proceed to the next dogtooth.

6. Finish the end of the binding in the same way as the beginning. Repeat for the remaining sides.

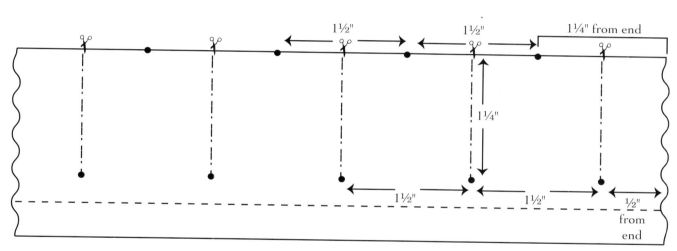

Marking the Dogtooth Binding

NORTH, EAST, SOUTH & WEST, MY CAPTAIN IS THE BEST, 76" x 81", 1996. Made by the author for her husband, John, who loves sailing. After three sailboats, Linda was still a landlubber, so John opted for the tandem (symbolized in the center appliqué) he now captains.

Fabric Requirements

Pattern piece yardages given assuming no fabric will be repeated in another compass.

5 yards background material
5 yards for waves
2¼" x 330" binding (eight 2¼" x 44" strips), extra
   yardage from background waves can be used
⅛ yard for A
¼ yard for B
¼ yard for C
¼ yard for D
¼ yard for E
¼ yard for F
¼ yard for G
½ yard for H
¼ yard for I
¼ yard for J

Supplies

Basic sewing kit, page 21
1⁄16" hole punch (optional)
Batting for 76" x 81" quilt top
Backing for 76" x 81" quilt top

The main pattern in this quilt, designed for machine piecing, is a 24" Mariner's Compass. It was my first attempt at machine piecing. The novice to advanced machine-piecing quilter can produce a wonderful Mariner's Compass quilt by making four 42" blocks with wave borders.

Adding an original center appliqué can create a personal touch. The template can be free-hand drawn or traced from a projected picture on a wall. Just transfer the tracings onto template plastic and cut out.

The pattern includes instructions for a 4-, 8-, 16-, or 32-point compass. The same compass may be used for each block, alternated, or one of each. All the compasses fit together in the same way, with the larger pieces breaking into smaller pieced units as more points are added.

Cutting Instructions

Make plastic templates and trace around them on the wrong side of the fabric, except for the wave templates that are to be appliquéd to the 42½" compasses. Mark the sewing line by drawing a dot on the fabric inside the 1⁄16" template holes. The dots are the pinning and sewing line guides.

(4) 42½" blocks from background fabric
(4) 42½" blocks from wave fabric

4-Pt Compass
(8) A pieces
(4) B pieces
(32) F pieces
(32) G pieces
*(4) J and Jr pieces

8-Pt Compass
(8) A pieces
(8) B pieces
(32) F pieces
(32) G pieces
(8) H pieces

16-Pt Compass
(8) A pieces
(8) B pieces
(8) E pieces
(32) F pieces

(32) G pieces
(16) I pieces

32-Pt Compass
(8) A pieces
(8) B pieces
(32) C pieces
(16) D pieces
(8) E pieces
(32) F pieces
(32) G pieces

*Trace J on paper, flip on fold line, and trace Jr to make complete template. Trace on template plastic.

Hint: Cut fabrics for one compass at a time. Keeping track of 400 pieces divided between four different blocks can be unnecessarily intimidating.

Reminder: Seam allowances have been added to the templates. The dots, cut and marked as explained in Template Patterns, page 21, are the machine starting and stopping points.

Block Assembly
4-Point Mariner's Compass

Instructions are for one compass.

1. Sew two A pieces by matching the dots on the two long sides. Sew dot to dot. Repeat with three more A pairs. Join two A pairs. Repeat with remaining two units. Pin and sew halves making sure the center points match.

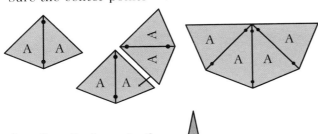

2. Sew four B pieces to the base of the north, east, south, and west A triangles.

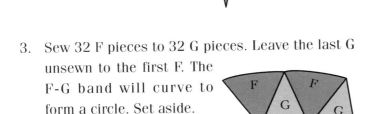

3. Sew 32 F pieces to 32 G pieces. Leave the last G unsewn to the first F. The F-G band will curve to form a circle. Set aside.

4. Sew the base of the J unit to base of northeast triangle A. Pin and sew from dot A to dot C. Then, pin and sew from dot A to dot B.

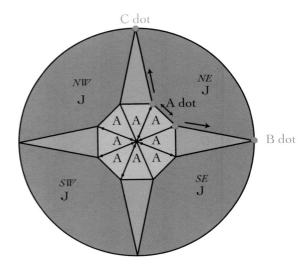

5. Repeat Step 4 for the remaining J units and sections of the compass.

6. Pick up the F-G band from Step 3. Starting with the north B tip, match dots and pin the last G, right sides together, to the left side tip of north B tip. Match the dots of eight G pieces between the north and west B tips around the edge of the northwest J unit. Continue around the remaining J unit sections. Sew with right sides together.

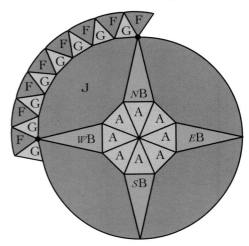

8-Point Mariner's Compass

1. Sew eight A pieces together as in Step 1, 4-Point Compass instructions.

2. Sew the base of each B to the base of each A.

3. Sew 32 F pieces and 32 G pieces together to create a curved band as in Step 3, page 116.

4. Pin and sew H from dot D to dot E. Then, pin and sew from dot D to dot F.

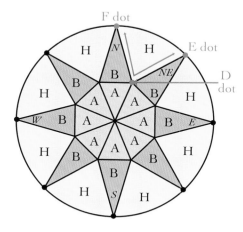

5. Repeat Step 4 for remaining H pieces.

6. Attach the F-G band beginning with the north B tip, working counterclockwise, matching the dots to the circle's H edges.

16-Point Mariner's Compass

1. Sew eight A's together as in Step 1, 4-Point Compass instructions.

2. Sew the base of each B to the base of each A.

3. Sew 32 F pieces to 32 G pieces, creating a curved band as in Step 3, page 116.

4. Sew an I to each side of an E. Repeat, making eight I-E-I units.

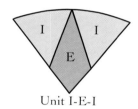

Unit I-E-I

5. Pin and sew from dot to dot, uniting one I-E-I unit to a B. Pin and sew from dot to dot, uniting the remaining side to the opposite B.

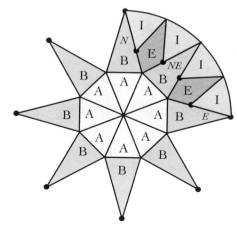

6. Attach the F-G band beginning with the north B tip, working counterclockwise and matching the dots to the circle's I edges.

32-Point Mariner's Compass

1. Sew eight A pieces together as in Step 1, 4-Point Compass instructions.

2. Sew the base of each B to the base of each A.

3. Sew 32 F pieces to 32 G pieces, creating a curved band as in Step 3, page 116.

4. With right sides together and matching dots, sew C to each side of D.

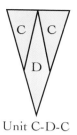

Unit C-D-C

5. Sew a C-D-C unit to each side of E, with the C-D-C unit replacing I used in Step 4 of the 16-Point Compass. Match dots, pin, and sew this new unit from dot to dot, as in Step 5, of the 16-point Mariner's Compass.

6. Attach the F-G band beginning with the north B tip, working counterclockwise and matching the dots to the circle's C edges.

Appliquéing to Background Block

1. Iron the block so that the center lies flat. There should be no ripples in the compass.

2. Fold the background block in half vertically and horizontally to find the center. Finger press.

3. Center the compass over the block and pin. Needle-turn the edges of the compass and appliqué in place.

Wave Border

1. Join the wave pattern sections and trace one-fourth of the wave section onto the right side of the 42½" block of the wave fabric, starting at the lower left corner. The template should extend from the left side center to the bottom center.

2. Flip the pattern over to trace the lower right corner. Continue flipping and tracing around the block.

3. Cut out the pattern about ⅛" from the lines for the needle-turn appliqué seam allowance.

4. Place and pin onto the Mariner's Compass block. Appliqué in place. Repeat for the other blocks.

Joining the Blocks

1. Sew the two finished blocks together.

2. Repeat with the remaining two blocks.

3. Match and pin the center seams, then sew the four blocks together.

Center Appliqué

The center appliqué is optional. An anchor, ship's wheel, crossed oars, or a canoe can continue the nautical theme.

1. Fold an 8½" x 11" or larger piece of paper in half and draw half of the object on the fold. Cut out.

2. Unfold and trace the pattern onto freezer paper. Transfer to the right side of the fabric.

3. Place on the quilt and needle-turn appliqué.

Finishing

1. Layer the backing, batting, and top. Baste.

2. Quilt as desired, or draw random squiggly lines across the background fabric to indicate waves. Echo quilt on and around the waves.

3. On the compasses, quilt down the center of the points. Use squiggly lines on pieces F and G. Outline quilt and center appliqué.

4. Apply the binding, following the general directions, page 23.

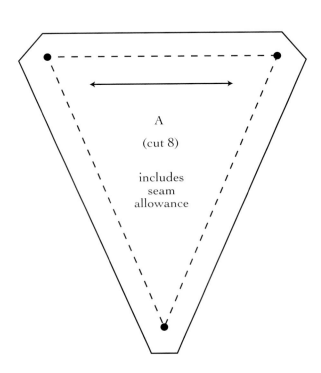

A
(cut 8)

includes
seam
allowance

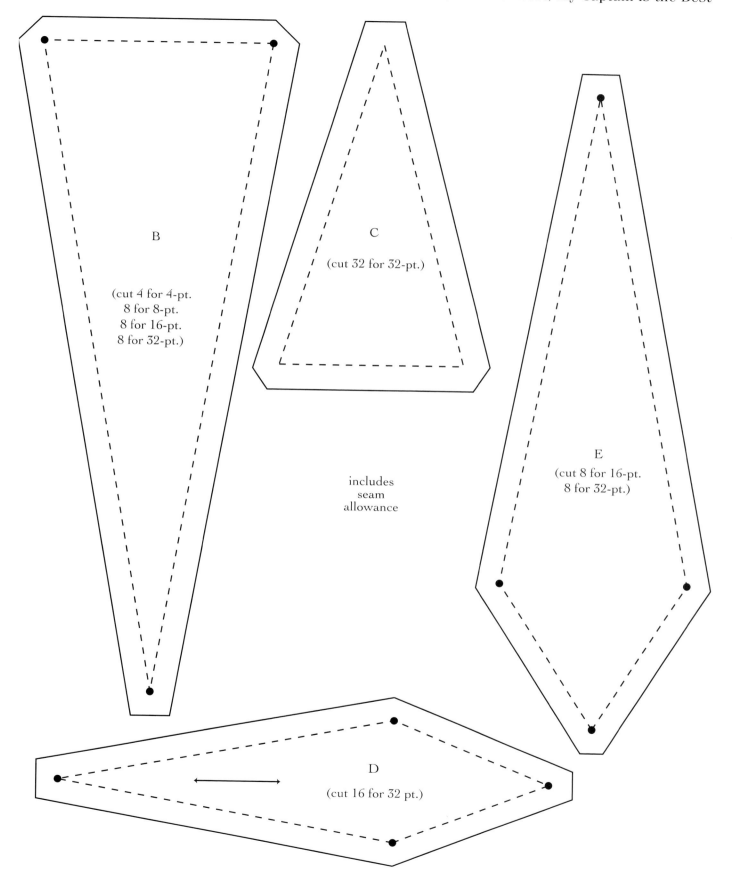

B

(cut 4 for 4-pt.
8 for 8-pt.
8 for 16-pt.
8 for 32-pt.)

C

(cut 32 for 32-pt.)

includes
seam
allowance

E
(cut 8 for 16-pt.
8 for 32-pt.)

D

(cut 16 for 32 pt.)

BEST OF FOUR BLOCKS...AND MORE *Linda Giesler Carlson*

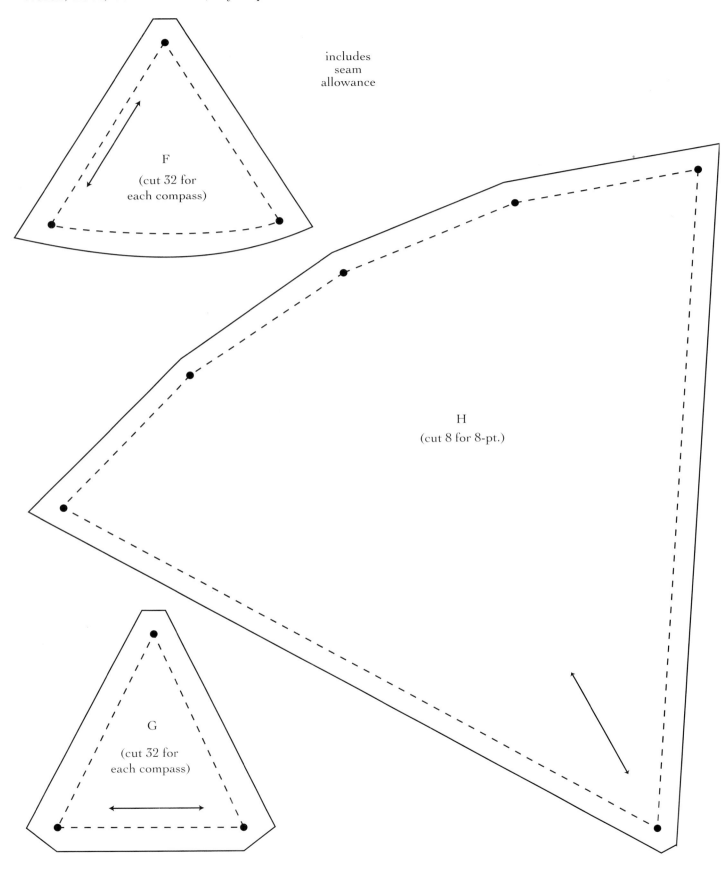

F

(cut 32 for
each compass)

includes
seam
allowance

H
(cut 8 for 8-pt.)

G

(cut 32 for
each compass)

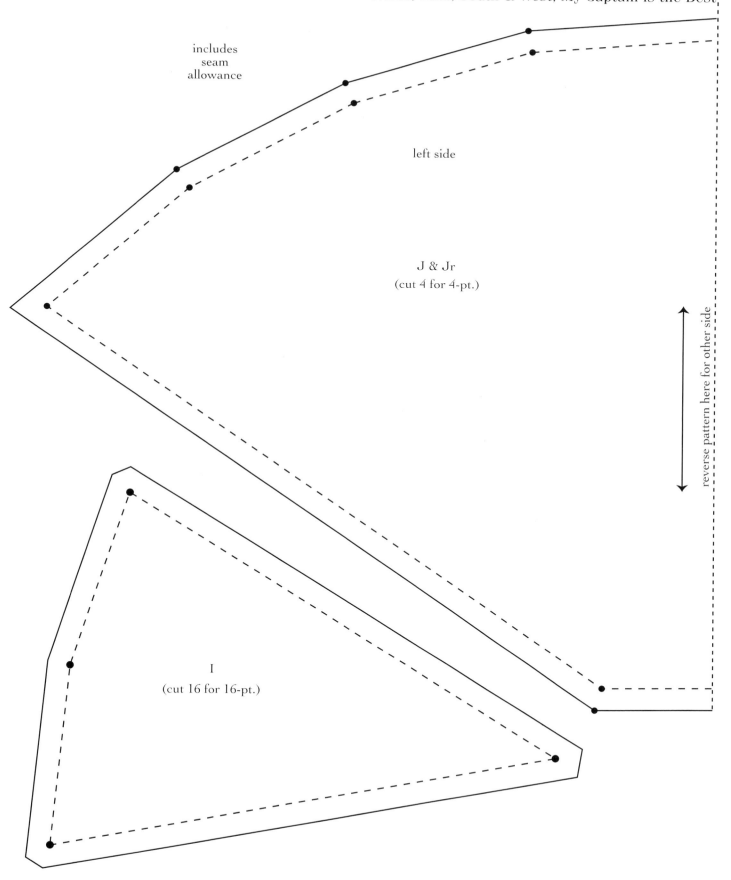

includes
seam
allowance

left side

J & Jr
(cut 4 for 4-pt.)

reverse pattern here for other side

I
(cut 16 for 16-pt.)

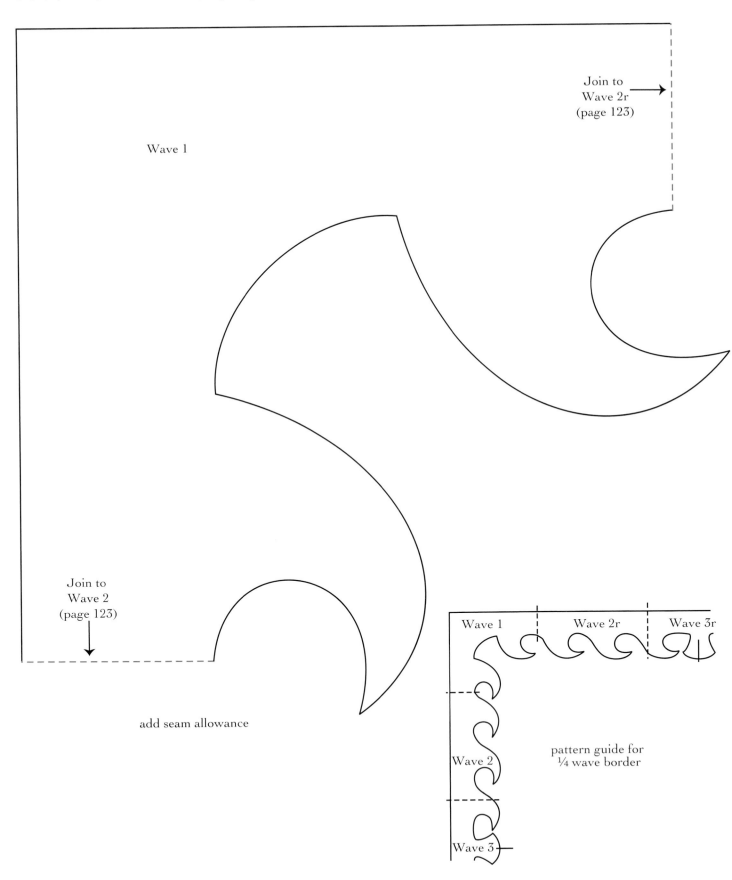

Wave 1

Join to
Wave 2r
(page 123)

Join to
Wave 2
(page 123)

add seam allowance

Wave 1   Wave 2r   Wave 3r

Wave 2

Wave 3

pattern guide for
¼ wave border

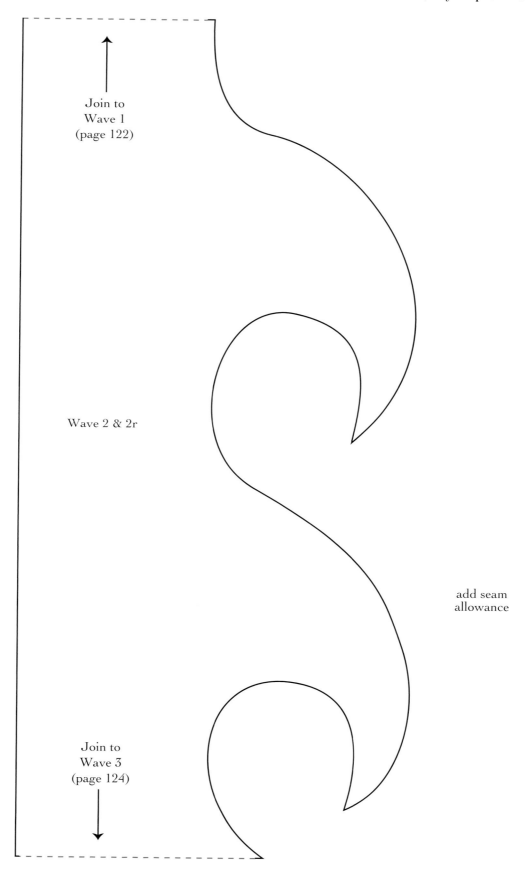

Join to
Wave 1
(page 122)

Wave 2 & 2r

add seam
allowance

Join to
Wave 3
(page 124)

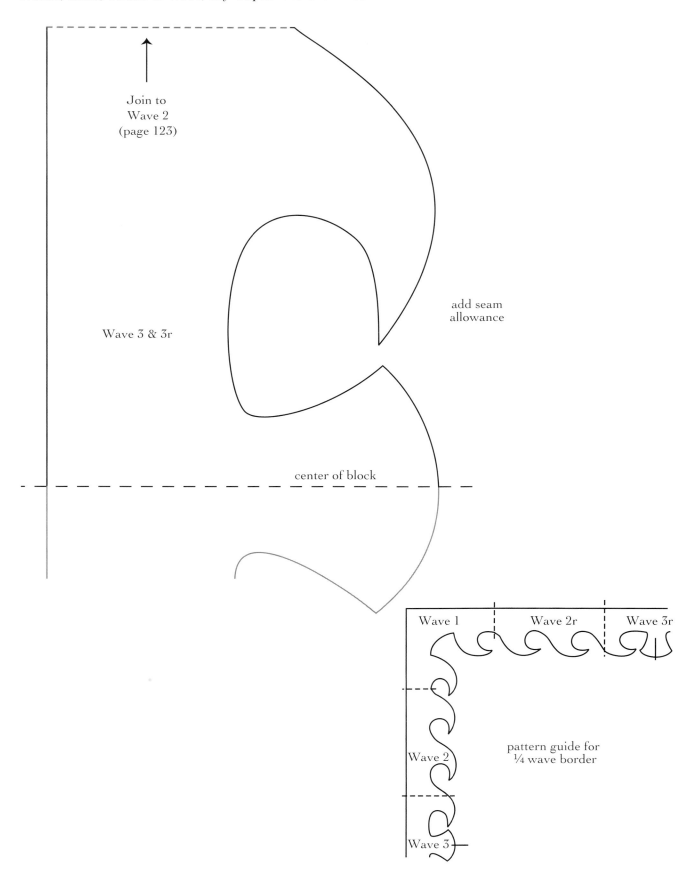

Join to
Wave 2
(page 123)

Wave 3 & 3r

add seam
allowance

center of block

Wave 1   Wave 2r   Wave 3r

Wave 2

pattern guide for
¼ wave border

Wave 3

Chapter 5

Findings of State
quilt documentation projects

Research Procedures

Beginning in 1989, I surveyed 30 state quilt search projects and 108 museum collections to determine whether large four-block pieced or appliquéd quilts were a natural progression from earlier whole-cloth and medallion quilt styles, and whether they had a regional origin. My research focused on the first 13 colonies and states admitted to the Union before 1850. Completed or ongoing documentation projects from 30 states and Washington, D.C. were reviewed. When state documentation was lacking, the largest museum collections were surveyed.

Of those state projects and museums responding to questionnaires, 407 of 46,563 quilts, or 0.87 percent, were constructed in the four-block style. An additional 105 quilts from private collections and 55 from museums were found and evaluated, bringing the total to 567 quilts, or 1.10 percent, which means about one in 90 quilts were made in the four-block style/set. Results showed this style/set occurred no earlier than whole-cloth and medallion quilts, but emerged during the early decades of the nineteenth century, as did quilts with nine or more smaller blocks repeated across the quilt top.

Findings

The following statistics pertain to the total quilts found within the 30 states, in addition to 108 museum collections within states where state project data were lacking. All types of quilts were included in the total count: whole-cloth, appliquéd, pieced, and tied. Therefore, the percentages are especially low. For example, Ohio found 140 appliquéd quilts made between 1834 and 1900. Because 70 were in the four-block style/set, the 50 percent rates seems high. But when compared to the total number of quilts (7,000) found of all styles/sets (including whole-cloth, medallion, multiple-block, or Log Cabin, etc.), the percentage of four-block quilts drops to 1 percent.

Sources and General Data			
	Quilts Found	**4-Block Quilts**	**Documented %**
State Projects	46,563	407	0.87
Museums	4,732	55	1.16
Private Collections	105	105	
Total	**51,400**	**567**	**1.10**

Significance: About 1 in 90 quilts made before 1900 was a four-block quilt.

Projects with the Most 4-Block Quilts

State	4-Block Quilts	Total Quilts	Documented %
Pennsylvania	123*	1,942	6.33
Ohio	70	7,000	1.00
Illinois	25	15,808	0.16
South Carolina	21	3,100	0.68
Georgia	25	6,373	0.39
Tennessee	11	1,425	0.77
Louisiana	10	1,850	0.54
Missouri	7	720	0.97
North Carolina	6	10,000	0.06
Kentucky	5†	600	0.83

* In March 1993, only 15 or 67 counties were complete. Today, many more are complete, but data were not available.
† 1,000 quilts documented, but only 600 documentation forms available for review.

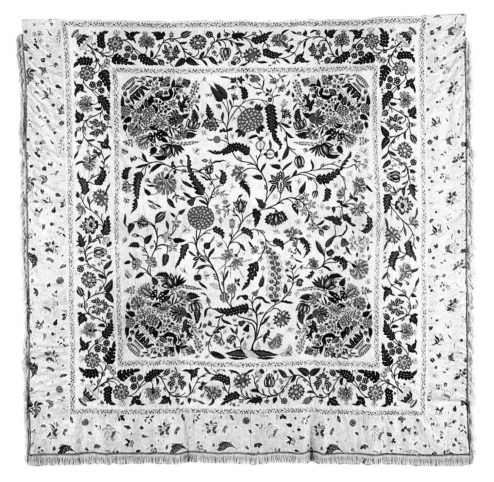

PALAMPORE-LIKE NEEDLEWORK SPREAD, 90" x 102", made in Masulipatam, India, ca. 1690–1700. Made of linen, cotton, and silk embroidery, this quilt has a definite quadrant feeling. The chintz border on three sides was added during the last half of the eighteenth century. The center and first border are embroidered with the chain stitch to be Palampore-like. Authentic Palampores were dye painted, especially with the Tree of Life design or other center motif. This piece was intended for the Dutch Holland export market and was bought in Europe by an American antiques dealer. Courtesy of Colonial Williamsburg Foundation.

American Four-Block Quiltmakers

Factors contributing to the emergence of this setting/style seem to be emigration and migration patterns, access to ports of trade, and economic circumstances. Early exploration of what finally became the first 13 English colonies was done independently by England, France, and Holland. Private trading and commercial venture companies, such as the Virginia Company of London, the Massachusetts Bay Company, and the Dutch West India Company, brought English families seeking the opportunity for religious freedom and land, in addition to Scots-Irish Protestants fleeing political and religious persecution. In the 1720s, these settlers began to be joined by thousands of German Lutherans, who brought with them a love of nature's beauty, bounty, and diversity, as well as the artistry and skills needed to produce Fraktur folk art.

My findings indicate that the large four-block appliqué quilt was more likely to have been constructed first and foremost by those of German descent, and secondly by Scots-Irish immigrants to Pennsylvania and the Carolinas or women influenced by the German Fraktur style of decoration.

As these people moved within the United States, their designs spread with them. The eighteenth to early nineteenth-century migration trails of Protestant Germans of Pennsylvania, Scots-Irish Presbyterians, some Quakers, and a few Catholics led to inland settlements in Ohio, Illinois, Tennessee, and Missouri, as well as to the Carolinas and Georgia on the eastern and southern seaboard. This is where, proportionately, many four-block quilts were found.

Dispersal/Growth of Four-Block Seeds

In addition to emigration and migration patterns, access to ports of trade and economic circumstances played an important role in the development of the four-block quilt style. In order for a large four-block quilt to be made, large pieces of fabrics had to be available. Only if quilters had access to a loom capable of weaving cloth 24" or more in width could they make a quilt with four large squares or rectangles, as well as even smaller blocks for an appliqué quilt. By 1689, seaports were established on almost the entire length of the East Coast at Plymouth, Chesapeake Bay, Hudson Bay, Delaware Bay, Charleston, and Savannah, making possible the import of textiles.

The textile industry in both America and England began to be mechanized by the last quarter of the eighteenth century. The cotton gin was invented in 1792–93, and machine-spun cotton thread in the early nineteenth century led to a decline of home-produced linen. Shortly after 1800, Ohio textile production became mechanized. Cloth production boomed by the 1830s. Still, between 1820 and 1860, one-third of all imports from England were textiles.[6]

England's East India Company had been supplying silks and cottons, but these items were so high in demand that attempts were made to produce them in western countries. England provided special bounties for planting mulberry trees, the fruit of which was to be used as food for the imported silkworm. Charters were issued for ventures in New Jersey, the Carolinas, and Georgia to produce silk for thread, but none were successful. Attempts were also made to create similar effects with domestic textiles. Woolen crewel yarn spun from sheep's wool was used for embroidering designs like those found on Indian prints.

In time, the problem was solved by changes in taste. Chintz cottons, which were relatively cheaper than silk, became stylish. Chintz whole-cloth, medallion style, or cut-out chintz appliqué quilts were the high-style bedroom furnishings of the New England and Atlantic seaboard states from about 1820, until they faded from glory around 1850. It appears that chintz and whole-cloth quilts may have been the predecessors of the four-block quilt, which soon spread its wings of diverse variation. The four-block style/set blossomed between the 1820s and 1870s. Medallion quilts continued to be made during the mid-nineteenth century, but waned in popularity as quiltmakers were ready to explore styles and sets other than whole-cloth and medallion.

People and fabrics moved about the country. The Midwest became an alluvial plain of sorts where the three colonial cultural regions came together: New England, the Midlands, and the South. Scots-Irish Presbyterian settlers came via the Pennsylvania (Forbes) Road, continuing by boat. New England migrants from Connecticut, Massachusetts, and Vermont traveled to the Western or Connecticut Reserve further inland. Once the Ohio-Erie Canal was built between 1825 and 1832, Irish and German canal laborers became permanent settlers.[7] All Americans' lives changed when the Baltimore-Ohio (B&O) Railroad charter was issued in 1827. Only freight was carried at first, then passengers in 1859. To Native Americans, it was the "iron horse" that belched smoke. To frontier quilters and general store proprietors, it was the mail-order fabric store.

When quilters couldn't or didn't weave their background material, they bought it from a merchant, if economically feasible, provided he could get it. Relatively easy access to ports of trade would naturally keep the merchant's transportation expenses down. Flatboats and barges on navigable interior rivers were the only access some people had to yard goods.

Ohio quilters benefited from ever-expanding road systems stretching across the state.[8] Originating in the Conestoga Creek region of Lancaster County, Pennsylvania, during the eighteenth century, the horse-drawn freight Conestoga wagon could carry up to six tons of merchandise. It was the forerunner of the Prairie Schooner wagon that brought thousands of immigrants to the inland states. The Pennsylvania (Forbes) Road provided access to the western frontier, which was Ohio and beyond.

Established by 1760, the Great Wagon Road, starting at the Schuylkill River in Philadelphia, was used by most of the first German immigrants going to North Carolina in the mid 1800s. After 1725, available land in Pennsylvania was scarce, so a southern migration developed. This 735-mile road crossed the Susquehanna River, passed through Maryland, Virginia, North Carolina, and South Carolina, then followed the Savannah River in Augusta, Georgia.[9]

By 1817, the Cumberland or National Road was complete from northwest Maryland through southwest Pennsylvania to the Ohio border at Wheeling, West Virginia. By the late 1830s, women in southwest Springfield, Ohio, had much easier access to fabric. The Cumberland Gap, located near the point where Kentucky, Virginia, and Tennessee meet, was where Daniel Boone blazed the Wilderness Road in 1769.

Even in America's pre-Revolutionary years, East Coast and Mid-Atlantic immigrants sought the free, fertile lands of the interior. Crossing the Allegheny Mountains through the Cumberland Gap made migration possible all the way to the Mississippi River and opened the Northwest Territory to settlement. Besides this route to the interior, early French emigrés came to the Louisville, Kentucky, area from the South via the Mississippi River at New Orleans.

After 1776, the Ohio River brought many German migrants from New England and the Mid-Atlantic states through Pittsburgh. The importance of the Ohio and Mississippi rivers in providing an exchange of goods from the northeastern states to the Gulf of Mexico and back is paramount. In my study, I discovered inland quilts with similar characteristics that had documented provenance indicating they had been made hundreds of miles apart. It wasn't until the Louisiana Purchase in 1803 that future midwestern states would benefit from the Missouri River connection to trade centers in our country and abroad.

Chapter 6

States with Several
four-block quilts

Pennsylvania
Commemorative Four-Block Eagle Quilts

William Penn received his charter in 1681 from King Charles II to settle the region of Pennsylvania. He brought a group of Quakers seeking to establish a colony based on a government of popular will and religious tolerance. Experiments in democratic forms of government encouraged other ethnic immigrants to settle in Pennsylvania in large blocks. Rhineland and southern Germans settled in great numbers in the inland counties of Lancaster, Lehigh Berks, and Northampton.

English, Scots-Irish, French, Welsh, Cornish, and Irish also settled the state, but by the the American Revolution, one-third of the state was populated by German settlers, who were so numerous they became known as the Pennsylvania Dutch (*Deutsche*). Some integrated well into area communities; others wanted to settle in counties west of the English and German areas. This group settled along the western frontier. By this time it had quickly become a keystone area, first integrating the older colonies of the Northeast and the South, and later the states of the East with the developing territories and states of the Midwest. Along with developing road systems, the three major ports of call were at Philadelphia, Pittsburgh, and Erie, with the Delaware, Susquehanna, Allegheny, Monongahela, and Ohio rivers used as supplemental connections throughout the state and beyond its borders in all directions. This provided transportation of yard goods, as well as other necessities.

As previously stated, quilters of Pennsylvania German heritage in this study made more quilts in the four-block style/set than their counterparts in other states. Common Pennsylvania-German quilt characteristics were hanging-diamond background crosshatching; brightly colored backgrounds, often orange-yellow instead of white; undulating, quilted, or appliquéd feather vines in borders or appliquéd vines with flowers; buds and/or birds; eight-pointed stars; Fraktur-style tulips; fruits of nature – oak leaves, trees, urns of flowers; and an inner border of triangles, or often just a narrow unpieced border, to define the four-block center field (see PHILADELPHIA CENTENNIAL EAGLE, page 101).

Oak leaves, either quilted or appliquéd, symbolized happiness, stability, and long life. In *Plain & Fancy: Country Quilts of the Pennsylvania-Germans*, Anita Schorsch believes Western culture holds them as a symbol of life, a gift of grace either as the Old Testament Tree of Knowledge or the New Testament Tree of Life. Usage of the dove meant the Holy Spirit of the Trinity or the Annunciation of Mary whereas the eagle was to bring believers closer to God. Quilts incorporating the rose or lily, tulip, as it was later known, was a symbol for Mary.[10] During Martin Luther's Reformation, the heart became a predominant symbol for abundance. Pennsylvania-Germans felt the heart represented divine and amorous love and often reserved the motif for the bridal quilt.

A special design unique to Pennsylvania must be recognized. The Eagle quilts found primarily in Pennsylvania were most likely made to commemorate our country's first centennial through Philadelphia's Centennial Exposition in 1876. Historian Ruth Finley found some of these quilts were called Union and suggested that the single Eagle pattern was fleetingly revived by northern sympathizers in the

1860s from the Eagle quilt predecessors of the Revolutionary War. In actuality, the few Lone Eagle quilts found before 1860 were probably patriotic responses to the Mexican War of 1846–1848. Only one four-block Eagle quilt from Pennsylvania found in this survey was made between 1860 and 1865. The other ten were made between 1870 and 1890. Eleven four-block Eagle quilts found were from Pennsylvania, three were from Ohio, and one was from New Jersey.

Stencil or Cut-out Appliqué Designs

The German art of ornamental paper cutting, scherenschnitte, became an original source for beautiful cutout appliqué patterns. Tinkers, traveling tin salesmen, could pay for a night's dinner and lodging with a pierced and cut tin stencil, paper cutwork appliqué patterns, or quilting stencils.

Ohio
Red and Green Four-Block Quilts

Quilts in Community: Ohio's Traditions (Rutledge Hill Press, 1991) was written after the project document-ed 7,000 quilts. In the chapter "German Aesthetics, Germanic Communities," Ricky Clark reveals that about one-half of the 140 appliqué quilts found in the Ohio project made between 1834 and 1900 were in the quadrant, four-block style/setting. Migrating Pennsylvania-German Protestants and some Catholics popularized red and green floral appliqué in mid-nineteenth-century Ohio. The style/setting most favored included wide multiple borders around the center area, ending frequently with a high-contrasting colorful binding. Floral appliqué reached its peak in Ohio between 1850 and 1860.

Statistics show that of the 140 appliqué quilts made between 1834 and 1900, 42 quilts, or 30 percent, were made by German immigrants or first-generation Americans. Of 74 quilts with the ethnic background of the maker known, 42 quilts, or 57 percent, were made by Germanic women. These statistics are especially meaningful when considering the 1850 census. Only 6 percent of the population were immigrants from Germany, and 10 percent were Germans from Pennsylvania.

Border and block motifs of a Pennsylvania quilt top, ca. 1845, featuring scherenschnitte and tinker-cut patterns. From the author's collection.

Star Spangled Banner, 72½" x 74½", ca. 1875. Made by a member of the Veley family of Bowling Green, Ohio. This stunning red, white, and blue four-block quilt, owned by an aunt of Ohio resident Anita Shackelford, represents a numerical nightmare. The author owns a nine-block quilt of this pattern. Photo by Anita Shackelford.

Illinois

Canals, Lakes, Rivers, and Roads Bring Four-Block Quiltmakers

The area we now know as Illinois was controlled by France until 1763, when Great Britain gained control after the French and Indian wars. With the 1779 capture of the British seat of government in Kaskaskia, Illinois became a county of Virginia. After first being part of the Northwest Territory, then the Indiana Territory, the Illinois Territory finally gained statehood in 1818. Very early Anglo-Saxon British Isles settlers came from Virginia, Kentucky, and Tennessee to southern Illinois. Northwestern Germans immigrated to Illinois and Missouri as early as 1832. According to Cheryl Wieburg Kennedy, director of the Early American Museum of Mahomet, Illinois, and the Illinois Quilt Research Project, many 1840s northern Illinois communities were settled by direct German immigrants and Pennsylvania-Germans who had come from Pennsylvania, North Carolina, and Ohio via the Erie Canal, the Great Lakes, the Ohio River, and the National Road. Other New Englanders and New Yorkers of Scots-Irish descent also came by this northern route.

The Royal area (Champaign County), German Valley, Stephenson County, southeastern Wabash County, and Emden are among many other areas and communities that were settled by German families. Many came not only for the freedom to enjoy political or religious beliefs, but for simple economic opportunities, including freedom from unstable financial conditions, overwhelming taxes, agricultural and industrial depression, and poor labor wages. English, Scots, and Welsh immigrants cited the latter reasons, while the Irish and lower Rhineland Germans added famine to the list because of the late 1840s potato crop failure.

During one three-year period in the early 1850s, more than 500,000 Germans immigrated to America, resulting in a 1.5 percent reduction in Germany's population. Even today, many family names can be traced back to the East Frisiam (Ostfiesen) area of Germany, as well as to the Rhine Valley. Documentation papers from the Illinois Quilt Research Project revealed that many mid-nineteenth-century Illinois residents could trace their families back to Pennsylvania. The 1860 Illinois Census reported that more than 80,000 Pennsylvanians had moved to Illinois.[11] In the 1840s, the vast European emigration began and continued through World War I.

South Carolina

Originality in Feathers, Roses, and Pineapples

Charleston, South Carolina, and Georgia quiltmakers had a greater supply of fabrics to choose from because South Carolina's coastline accommodated large ships. Charleston was a port of entry for countless immigrants; first English, then largely Scots-Irish and German. In *Social Fabric: South Carolina's Traditional Quilts* by Laurel Horton and Lynn Robertson Myers, Horton's chapter, "Quiltmaking Traditions in South Carolina," agrees with the findings of a Missouri quilt research historian, Suellen Meyer. In "Characteristics of Missouri-German Quilts" from *Uncoverings 1984*, Meyer said that even though there were outside influences on the traditions of the settled German community, these quiltmakers continued to use certain recognizable German characteristics, such as predilection toward all-over visual designs even when using a block pattern, a strong preference for designs with diagonal lines, a marked orderliness even when using many different fabrics, and a preference for yellow as a unifying color.[12]

Other European ethnic groups were represented, but here as well as along the Virginia coast, cultural heritages of the West Indies and especially of Africa became significant factors in the amount of leisure time a woman had to pursue quiltmaking. According to Horton, an assimilation of ethnic German and

Scots-Irish aesthetic principles is the reason why the German-occupied, Piedmont area quilts differ from those of the coastal plain. With Horton's help, 32 four-block quilts were found in the South Carolina project, 21 of which fell within my cut-off date of 1900. These 32 quilts show more original interpretations of commonly seen four-block patterns, such as the Princess Feather and Whig Rose.

An original Pineapple pattern was found to be very regional with three other extremely similar documented quilts within South Carolina, and six in other states: one each in Alabama, Virginia, Georgia, and Mississippi, and two in Texas. The Alabama pineap-

ple version is known as Alabama Beauty (see page 36 in *Roots, Feathers & Blooms*, AQS, 1994). The author's collection includes a much simpler version. More pieced four-block quilts (11) were found here than in any other state, with the possible exception of Pennsylvania.

Georgia and the Southern Coastal States

Georgia was the youngest of the first 13 colonies, in that England claimed the territory but did not effectively settle there until 1732. It was much larger then, as it included most of our present-day states of Alabama and Mississippi.

PINEAPPLE APPLIQUÉ, 75" x 75", made in South Carolina in 1840. Purchased by the author in Iowa. Pencil lines on the quilting are still visible, which means it has never been washed. Quilted with the Double Clamshell pattern. Photo by Richard Walker.

Austria-Bavarian (Salzburg) Germans settled in New Ebenezer and Savannah, Georgia, while the Scottish Highlanders went to Darien and New England Congregationalists went to Sundury and Midway. The Atlantic Ocean coastline had the most settlements by 1752. In the early decades of the 1800s, when plantations were firmly established, the Savannah summers, with their beastly temperatures and humidity, became vacation time for wealthy families to go to the southern highlands or northern cities of Boston, New York, or Philadelphia. Vacationing several weeks "up north" most likely afforded the opportunity to exchange and copy four-block patterns.[13] Anita Weinraub, the Georgia quilt documentation project director, has commented that there is still a strong Scots-Irish Presbyterian heritage within the state, followed secondly by a Baptist heritage.

Alas, very few large four-block quilts were found in Mississippi and Alabama. Considering the Louisiana project found about 10 and Georgia about 25, as yet, there is no plausible explanation other than that migrating Pennsylvania and South Carolina Germans and Scots-Irish didn't settle or stay long in these areas. It should be noted that when Georgia was admitted to the Union in 1783, Mississippi and Alabama were considered "Territories South of the Ohio River." They had been given to England by the 1763 Treaty of Paris at the end of the French and Indian wars. In the 1770s, both future states were greatly populated by migrant settlers seeking refuge from the ever-growing unrest with the British Crown rule on the eastern seaboard. Since 1682, France had long claimed New Orleans as a port of entry.

In 1731, Louisiana became a French crown colony. Besides French settlers, thousands of Germans settled on the river just above New Orleans in an area known as the German Coast. In a secret treaty of 1762, Louisiana and New Orleans were ceded to Spain. By 1783, Spain controlled most of the remaining Louisiana Territory, which encompassed nearly all areas west of the Mississippi River. In 1800, Spain ceded this vast area back to France. It was only three years later that President Thomas Jefferson authorized the Louisiana Purchase to expand America's holding.[14]

Louisiana held a strategic command on commerce within the interior, simply because the Mississippi River, draining the continental interior, flowed through there to the Gulf of Mexico. This one geographical fact had great impact on quilting in the Midwest: quiltmakers' choice of fabric was based on financial circumstances and availability of materials. After availability, choices of patterns were determined by need for a utilitarian or fancy quilt. If need allowed a special fancy quilt, then originality, personal ethnic heritage, or a neighbor's influential heritage largely determined the pattern to be used.

Tennessee
"Tinker" Stencil-Cut, Four-Block Appliqués

Virginians were the first émigrés led into this part of what was formerly western North Carolina by Thomas Walker in 1750. William Bean was the first permanent white settler to build his cabin along the Watauga River in 1768. By 1780, Nashborough (Nashville) was established. North Carolina finally ceded the territory to the United States government in 1789.

Morristown, Tennessee, was settled by Scots-Irish immigrants. They came down the Holston River from the Cumberland Gap. If they turned north, they went into Kentucky; if they turned south, they went to Morristown. Some Pennsylvania Germans came after the Civil War. Perhaps Germantown, Tennessee, was named by settlers from Germantown, Pennsylvania. By 1789, hundreds of settlers were coming into the area. The Revolutionary War was over, and some were ready to strike out for new lands; the land bonuses and lotteries given as payment for some who took part in the war had not proven successful. They were ready to try again.

Physically, Tennessee stretches from the Appalachian Mountain boundary with North Carolina in the east all the way to where the Mississippi River borders Missouri and Arkansas. It tended to be a state through which people migrated. Only 112 miles wide, people in Kentucky, Virginia, Georgia, Alabama, and Mississippi readily passed through (see KENTUCKY TOBACCO LEAF AND TULIP STENCIL QUILT below).

Perhaps Tennessee's migrant-oriented nature explains why it was not affected much by the European immigrant waves during the second- to third-quarter of the nineteenth century.

Missouri
The New Rhineland for Immigrating Germans

Ste. Genevieve was the first Missouri settlement established by French explorers in 1735, followed by Pierre Laclede from New Orleans 30 years later at St. Louis. Marthasville was the first settled village established in what was to become Warren County (west of St.

KENTUCKY TOBACCO LEAF AND TULIP STENCIL QUILT. 74" x 77½", made in Kentucky ca. mid-1800s. Purchased by the author in Iowa. Photo by Richard Walker.

Louis). The famous fur trader, Indian Phillips, came as an employee of a fur company in 1763, followed by Choteau and Lozie, who received grants from the Spanish government for a large tract of land in the present counties of Warren and St. Charles. Daniel Boone's son-in-law, Flanders Callaway, bought the grants, and in 1795, he established Callaway Post several miles west of Marthasville. Settlements in central Warren County date back to 1808, with the coming of Thomas Kennedy of Virginia, Anthony Keeler of Pennsylvania, Samuel Gibson of South Carolina, and Daniel McCoy and David Boyd of Kentucky.[15] In this pioneer period, Marthasville was the principal landing place for all the territory. It was the only avenue of marketing by boat for receiving goods and exporting farmers' produce. This shipping interest was a big business for the area.[16] Cotton was successfully raised, and it produced some of the clothing needs of the families. Flax was grown, chiefly for the bark of which linen and linsey were made. "A flax patch and a flock of sheep were the pride of every family, and the lady who was an expert flax spinner and weaver was the envy of her sex, and had the admiration of the opposite sex."[17]

By the time of the Louisiana Purchase from France in 1803, among the 10,000 French settlers from Illinois country were Virginians and émigrés from Kentucky and Tennessee, who then became the major immediate source for continued settlement until 1820. Immigrants came from Germany, Ireland, and England via the Mississippi River. In about 1824, Gottfried Duden thoroughly traveled through the Warren County area. When Duden returned to Germany, he wrote a book so accurately describing what he had seen that when immigrants settled in this area, they already knew many places and scenes.

Some societies came to Missouri *en masse*, such as the Berlin Society in 1833 to St. Charles, followed by the Gissen Society in 1834. "No other class of people ever did more for the development of the country, or made better or more thrifty citizens than the Germans. They caused the hillsides to blossom with fruit and opened large farms in the midst of the dense forest. Villages and towns sprang up where solitude had reigned, and the liberal arts began to flourish."[18] The greatest influx of German immigrants to Marthasville began in 1834, principally from New Orleans up the Mississippi River.

The German Settlement Society of Pennsylvania was organized in Philadelphia on August 27, 1863, for the purpose of founding a German colony where language and customs could be preserved in the new country. Scouts were sent out to locate suitable areas. George F. Bayer was the agent hired to buy land, lay out the town, and start the new colony of Hermann (later to become Hermann, Missouri, in Gasconade County).[19] My paternal great-grandparents, John Gerhard Spoede (Spöde is the German spelling) and his new bride of three weeks, Anna M. Siltmann, made the journey from New Orleans to St. Louis, Missouri, in September 1855.

By the beginning of the Civil War in 1860, so many Germans had settled on the bluffs and uplands south of the Missouri River, as well as in St. Louis and further west, that the area became known as the Missouri Rhineland. In "Characteristics of Missouri-

Anna M. Siltmann Spoede, 1835–1910. The author's paternal great-great grandmother spinning wool.

German Quilts," Suellen Meyer's article in *Uncoverings 1984* (American Quilt Study Group, 1985), she discovered distinctive styles and characteristics of Missouri-German-made quilts from communities along the lower Missouri River that had been settled virtually by German immigrants alone.

During the next decade, more immigrants came from Ohio, Illinois, and Indiana than from the upper South. Still more Germans came, settling this time in Kansas City, as well as in St. Louis. Like Tennessee, Missouri saw many migrant populations pass through its borders, which touch Iowa, Illinois, Kentucky, Tennessee, Arkansas, Oklahoma, Kansas, and Nebraska.

Until Texas was admitted to the Union in 1845, Missouri was the westernmost state. For decades it served as the beginning of the Sante Fe and Oregon trails, bringing tens of thousands of explorers and settlers deeper into the frontier. St. Louis was the new western frontier's only contact with the culture of the East, while easterners thought of Missouri as the Gateway to the West. Throughout Missouri's early years of settlement and after, the importance of being bordered and transgressed by the Mississippi and Missouri rivers respectively allowed not only the east to meet the west, but the north to meet the south. Headwaters of the Mississippi begin in Minnesota in Itasca State Park and drain into the Gulf of Mexico. With its headwaters in Oregon, the Missouri River flows halfway across the United States before converging with the Mississippi on the Missouri-Illinois border. The Ohio River starts in Pennsylvania and converges with the Mississippi at the point where Missouri borders Illinois and Kentucky.

North Carolina
Princess Feather Pattern Preferred in Southwest Piedmont

North Carolina did not have a safe coastline or a large harbor to accept many European immigrants and trade ships from the Caribbean. Therefore, its first settlers in 1610 were Englishmen migrating south from the greatly expanding Jamestown, Virginia colony to take advantage of the rich bottomlands of the Carolinas. Trade products at this time could only move north into Virginia and New England to be sold or reshipped to world markets. Small, shallow, English keel ships could dock at Petersburg or Norfolk, Virginia.

By 1663, French, German, and Swiss colonists were migrating from Virginia and the Albemarle region of North Carolina, south down the Pamlico and Neuse rivers. After 1718, when Indian and pirate threats had been quelled, the lower Cape Fear region became home to migrants from Charleston, South Carolina, which was a major port of debarkation for European, Caribbean, and African immigrants.

The upper Cape Fear area of Campbelltown (now Fayetteville) was settled by thousands of Scottish immigrants fleeing British persecution after the ill-fated 40-minute Battle of Culloden in 1746. By 1750, migration from Philadelphia toward the interior Piedmont region was led by large populations of Protestant Germans and Scots-Irish Presbyterians who fled religious persecution in Germany and Ulster (Northern Ireland). Finding very little and costly land prompted them to venture south. This arduous migration trail, aptly named the Great Road, started in Philadelphia, Pennsylvania, and ended in the North Carolina counties of Yadking, Catawba, Person, and Pender via the headwaters of the Yadkin, Catawba, and Neuse rivers. Trade to and from these interior settlements was accomplished through Charleston, South Carolina; Augusta, Georgia; Knoxville, Tennessee; Baltimore; and Philadelphia. The population in 1760 totaled 130,000, with a breakdown of ethnic groups as follows: 45,000 English, 40,000 Scots, and 15,000 Germans.[20]

Eventually, the Scots-Irish became the largest ethnic group. The many thousands of German immigrants after 1790 didn't readily settle in North Carolina. Instead, they went on to the Midwest and larger cities from about 1830 to 1850. The use of the German language itself and the resulting isolation it caused were largely responsible for this migration. However, those families that stayed learned English around 1825.[21] Despite their language barriers, the German quiltmakers evidently influenced the Scots-Irish quiltmakers here in at least one pattern and setting – the four-block Princess Feather.

Perhaps the comparatively small number of Germans versus the other ethnic populations explains why approximately only 1 in 1,500 quilts made in North Carolina before 1900 were in the four-block style/set. In her article in *Bits and Pieces – Textile Traditions* (Oral Traditions Project, 1991), Kathleen Sullivan offers other valid reasons for German influence on North Carolina's quiltmaking, which in the case of the four-block quilt might account for its rarity in North Carolina.[22]

The earliest surviving documented North Carolina Project quilts were chintz, either the cut-out, pieced, or appliquéd medallion style. They came from the Piedmont counties, Mecklenburg, Carbarrus, Iredell, Davie, and McDowell. Mecklenburg was the center for Scots-Irish settlements. The height of popularity for this style of quilt was from 1820 to about 1850. As noted in Laurel Horton's thesis, "Economic Influences on German

MENNONITE ROSE AND TULIP LEAF WITH GRAPES, 88" x 88", 1890. Made in Elizabethtown, Pennsylvania. From the author's collection.

and Scots-Irish Quilts in Antebellunm Rown County, North Carolina" (Chapel Hill, 1979), some quilts made in North Carolina German communities settled before 1860 had decidedly different appearances from quilts made by Scots-Irish descendants in neighboring counties.[23] During this period before the Civil War, square blocks of repeated appliqués emerged as a new style, and so did the four-block quadrant arrangement.

No matter whether they came as immigrants from Europe or migrants from Pennsylvania or South Carolina, women of all ages surely admired one another's quilts, exchanged patterns, and remembered favorite quilts of their grandmothers for later reproduction to help alleviate the arduous, tedious days and months of traveling. This could account

for the fact that very similar quilts were found in counties separated by hundreds of miles. When several adjacent settlements (now counties) were populated by ethnic immigrants and migrants, the same reasoning holds true. For example, the North Carolina Project found more Princess Feather quilts originating in the southwest Piedmont counties of Cleveland, Gaston, Lincoln, and Catawba than anywhere else.

Kentucky
Political Battle Leaves Rose in the Middle
Native-born statesman Henry Clay and Kentucky-raised Zachary Taylor played a part in the often-used four-block pattern called Whig Rose or Democrat Rose. Clay was a staunch member of the Whig politi-

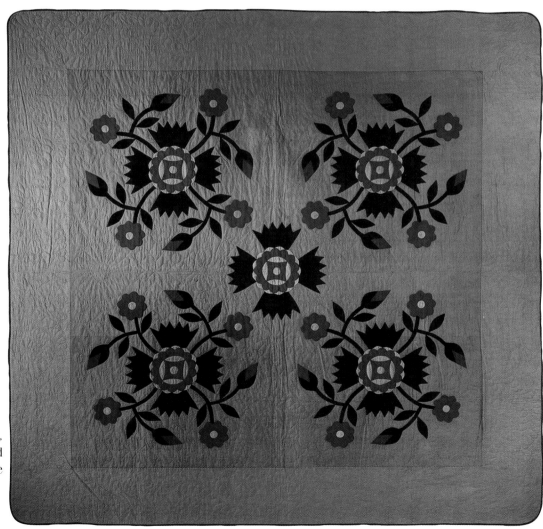

DEMOCRAT OR WHIG ROSE, 92" x 92", ca. 1865. Found in Pennsylvania. From the author's collection.

cal party from its infant beginnings to the party's formal organization in 1834. He opposed the federal Alien and Sedition Acts of 1798, the government's attempt to control criticism against slaveholders and businessmen by farmers who used the Mississippi River for transporting goods to New Orleans. It is possible that Kentucky women named this rose in honor of a native son arguing against slavery and for the well-being of the common man.

Democrat Andrew Jackson and Henry Clay were longtime political enemies. Since the War of 1812, Jackson had become a military hero. His native state was South Carolina before he worked in Nashville, Tennessee, as a lawyer prior to his military career. Could women from these states have named the same pattern Democrat Rose for their hero? By 1840, both names were commonly interchanged. But after Clay's defeat by Democrat James Polk in the Presidential election of 1844, a new pattern emerged named Whig's Defeat.

Closing Remarks

Rivers, trails, roads, then railroads moved people and goods across the entire continent. Quiltmakers didn't have to pack their ethnic heritage, but once they unpacked their large four-block quilts, it came through loud and clear. The beautiful German Fraktur designs applied with newly acquired English quilting skills brought memories to the Pennsylvania-German quiltmaker of a homeland far away. In their adopted homeland of America, their four-block quilts remain legacies of their German heritage.

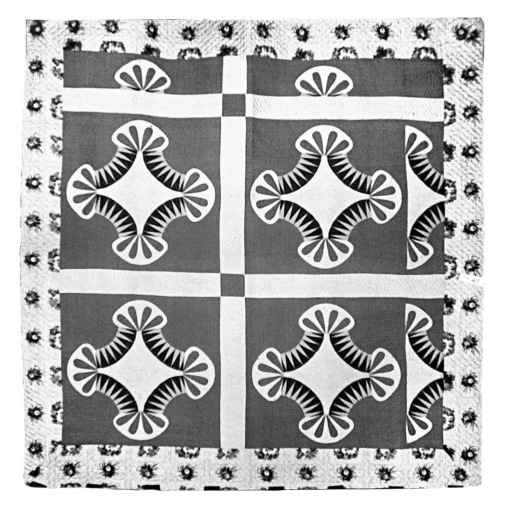

WHIG'S DEFEAT, 84" x 91", 1870. Made by Sarah Adeline Stewart. Her father came to Charleston in 1788, from Belfast, Ireland, as an infant. The family settled in upper South Carolina with other Scots-Irish immigrants where they farmed and ran a sawmill. Several quilts found by the survey may be classified as "transitional" because of their changing style – evidenced by the chintz border in this quilt and the lengthening of a four-block square quilt to a rectangle by adding two half blocks. None of the state projects or museums reported any four-block by two half blocks or six-block quilts made prior to their four-block quilts. Courtesy of the Folklife Resource Center, McKissick Museum, The University of South Carolina, Columbia, South Carolina.

1. Erma Hughes Kirkpatrick, "Garden Variety Quilts," *North Carolina Quilts* (Chapel Hill, N.C.: The University of North Carolina Press and London, 1988), p. 67.

2. Laurel Horton, "Textile Traditions in South Carolina's Dutch Fork," *Bits and Pieces – Textile Traditions* (Lewisburg, Penn.: Oral Traditions Project of the Union County Historical Society, Courthouse, 1991), p. 73.

3. For further information, refer to *New York Beauties: Quilts from the Empire State* by Atkins and Tepper, pp. 113–115.

4. *New Encyclopaedia Britannica*, Vol. 8, 1987.

5. Anita Schorsch, *Plain & Fancy: Country Quilts of the Pennsylvania-Germans* (New York: Sterling Publishing Co., Inc., 1992), p. 27.

6. Ellice Ronsheim, "The Impact of Technology on the Availability of Dress Goods in Ohio," *Quilts in Community: Ohio's Traditions* (Nashville, Tenn.: Rutledge Hill Press, 1991), pp. 57–60.

7. *New Encyclopaedia Britannica*, Vol. 29, 1987.

8. George W. Knepper, "Early Migrants to Ohio," *Quilts in Community: Ohio's Traditions*, pp. 9–10, 19.

9. Kathleen Sullivan, "Pieced and Plentiful," *Bits and Pieces – Textile Traditions*, p. 65.

10. Schorsch, *Plain & Fancy: Country Quilts of the Pennsylvania-Germans*, pp. 35–36.

11. Duane Elbert, *History from the Heartland: Quilt Paths Across Illinois* (Nashville, Tenn.: Rutledge Hill Press, 1993), pp. 23–25, 42, 43, and 49.

12. Suellen Meyer. "Characteristics of Missouri-German Quilts," *Uncoverings 1984* (Mill Valley, Calif.: American Quilt Study Group), pp. 105–111.

13. *New Encyclopaedia Britannica*, Vol. 8, 1987.

14. Ibid.

15. "Brief History of Warren County," *The Warrenton Banner*, Vol. L, No. 19, 18 Dec. 1914, p. 1.

16. "The First Town, Marthasville," *The Warrenton Banner*, Vol. L, No. 19, 18 Dec. 1914, p. 14.

17. "Chief Occupation," *The Warrenton Banner*, Vol. L, No. 19, 18 Dec. 1914, p. 4.

18. "The German Immigration," *The Warrenton Banner*, Vol. L, No. 19, 18 Dec. 1914, p. 2.

19. "Hermann Will Honor Its Founder in Kickoff at Town's Sesquicentennial," *The Warrenton News Journal*, No. 23, April 1986, p. B6.

20. Joyce Joines, "Making Do," *North Carolina Quilts*, pp. 9–10.

21. Kathleen Sullivan, *Bits and Pieces*, p. 68.

22. Ibid. pp. 69–70.

23. Laurel Horton, *Social Fabric: South Carolina's Traditional Quilts*, p. 20.

Bibliography

Allen, Rosemary E. *North Country Quilts and Coverlets from Beamish Museum, County Durham.* England: Beamish, 1987.

Arkansas Quilter's Guild, Inc. *Arkansas Quilts: Arkansas Warmth.* Kentucky: American Quilter's Society, 1987.

Atkins, Jacqueline M. and Phyllis A. Tepper. *New York Beauties: Quilts from the Empire State.* New York: Penguin Books USA., Inc., 1992.

Bishop, Robert. *New Discoveries in American Quilts.* New York: E. P. Dutton and Co., Inc., 1975.

Brackman, Barbara. *Clues in the Calico: A Guide to Identifying and Dating Antique Quilts.* Virginia: EPM Publishers, Inc., 1989.

Bresenhan, Karoline Patterson and Nancy O'Bryant Puentes. *Lone Stars – A Legacy of Texas Quilts, 1836–1936.* Texas: University of Texas Press, 1986.

Clark, Ricky, George Knepper, and Ellice Ronsheim. *Quilts in Community: Ohio's Traditions.* Tennessee: Rutledge Hill Press, 1991.

Cleveland, Richard L. and Donna Bister. *Plain and Fancy: Vermont's People and Their Quilts as a Reflection of America.* California: The Quilt Digest Press, 1991.

Elbert, Duane. *History from the Heartland: Quilt Paths across Illinois.* Tennessee: Rutledge Hill Press, 1993.

Finley, John. *Kentucky Quilts 1800–1900: The Kentucky Quilt Project.* New York: Pantheon Books, 1982.

Finley, Ruth. *Old Patchwork Quilts and the Women Who Made Them.* New York: Grosset and Dunlap, 1929.

Garoutte, Sally. *Uncoverings 1984: Volume 5 of the Research Papers of the American Quilt Study Group.* California: American Quilt Study Group, 1985.

Gwinner, Schnuppe von. *The History of the Patchwork Quilt – Origins, Traditions and Symbols of a Textile Art.* Pennsylvania: Schiffer Publishing Co., 1988.

Hall, Carrie and Rose Kretsinger. *The Romance of the Patchwork Quilt.* New York: Dover Publishers, Inc., 1988 ed.

Havig, Bettina. *Missouri Heritage Quilts.* Kentucky: American Quilter's Society, 1986.

Horton, Laurel and Lynn Robertson Myers. *Social Fabric: South Carolina's Traditional Quilts.* South Carolina: McKissick Museum, University of South Carolina, 1984.

Jenkins, Susan and Linda Seward. *The American Quilt Story – The How-To and Heritage of a Craft Tradition.* Pennsylvania: Rodale Press, 1991.

Lasansky, Jeanette, et al. *Bits and Pieces – Textile Traditions.* Pennsylvania: Oral Traditions Project of the Union County Historical Society, 1991.

MacDowell, Marsha and Ruth D. Fitzgerald, eds. *Michigan Quilts – 150 Years of a Textile Tradition.* Michigan: Michigan State University Museum, 1987.

Martin, Nancy. *Pieces of the Past.* Washington: That Patchwork Place, Inc., 1986.

Martin, Nancy. *Threads of Time.* Washington: That Patchwork Place, Inc., 1990.

Nelson, Cyril I. and Carter Houck. *Treasury of American Quilts.* New York: Greenwich House, 1982.

Peck, Amelia. *American Quilts and Coverlets in the Metropolitan Museum of Art.* New York: Dutton Studio Books, 1990.

Roberson, Ruth Haislip, ed., et al. *North Carolina Quilts.* North Carolina: The University of North Carolina Press and London, 1988.

Safford, Carleton L. and Robert Bishop. *America's Quilts and Coverlets.* New York: Bonanza Books, 1985.

Schorsch, Anita. *Plain & Fancy: Country Quilts of the Pennsylvania-Germans.* New York: Sterling Publishing Co., Inc., 1992.

Texas Heritage Quilt Society. *Texas Quilts – Texas Treasures.* Kentucky: American Quilter's Society, 1986.

Webster, Marie. *Quilts: Their Story and How to Make Them.* California: Practical Patchwork, 1990.

About The Author

Linda Giesler Carlson has always been inspired by her students' undiscovered talents. Her devotion to teaching quilting stems from her educational background, including two bachelor's degrees in education and a certification by the Library of Congress to transcribe braille. Through her teaching experience, Linda possesses a good sense of humor, patience, and flexibility, and allows her students to follow the creative beat of their own drum.

Since the 1980s, Linda has taught all areas of quiltmaking, specializing in appliqué and the history of and techniques in making large four-block quilts. She has taught throughout the United States for guilds, retreats, symposiums, and quilt shows such as the American Quilter's Society Show and Contest, the Quilt Odyssey, and the International Quilt Festival.

For the past 10 years, Linda has judged quilt shows, fairs, and contests both locally and nationally. She believes that judging helps her bring valuable information back to her students. Linda's own work and quilts from her collection have been featured in many exhibitions. About 30 quilts from her four-block collection were exhibited at the Museum of the American Quilter's Society in Paducah, Kentucky.

Linda has written four quilting books, as well as numerous articles for several national quilting magazines. In 1995, she presented a research paper on the roots of the large four-block quilt for a symposium at the Smithsonian Institution. In 1996, Linda received the G. Andy Runge Ambassador Award to recognize her representation of her hometown of Mexico, Missouri, during her teaching excursions.

Linda's workshops and lectures offer 27 classes featuring mostly hand appliqué and/or pieced quilt projects from large appliqué pieces to intricate scherenschnitte designs. Topics include machine projects, commemorative/memorial quilts, designing specific features for quilts such as feather borders, center and corner treatments, perfecting appliqué, 3-D techniques, and choosing background and quilting motifs. For more information on these classes, visit Linda's Web site at www.lindacarlsonquilts.com

Other AQS Books

This is only a small selection of the books available from the American Quilter's Society. AQS books are known worldwide for timely topics, clear writing, beautiful color photos, and accurate illustrations and patterns. The following books are available from your local bookseller, quilt shop, or public library.

#6292 us$24.95

#6414 us$25.95

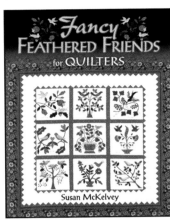

#6205 us$24.95

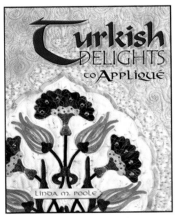

#6004 us$22.95

#6211 us$19.95

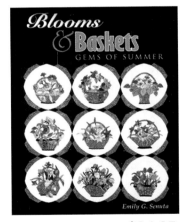

#5175 us$24.95

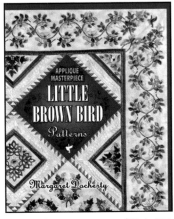

#5338 us$21.95

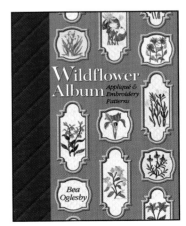

#5757 us$19.95

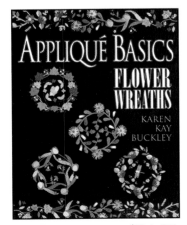

#5335 us$21.95